CULTURE IN IRELAND –

DIVISION OR DIVERSITY?

DEDICATION

This conference is dedicated to the example of Hubert Butler (1900–1991), a lifelong campaigner for cultural understanding and justice in Ireland and Europe.

'Living in social harmony is a most difficult art, the most absolute concentration is required, and perfect equilibrium. Our island is dangerously tilted towards England and towards Rome, good places in themselves, but best seen on the level.'
— Hubert Butler

Culture in Ireland–
Division or Diversity?

**Proceedings of the Cultures of Ireland
Group Conference, 27–28 September 1991**

Edited by Edna Longley

Institute of Irish Studies
The Queen's University of Belfast

ACKNOWLEDGEMENT

We are extremely grateful to the International Fund for Ireland for funding this book.

First published 1991
by the Institute of Irish Studies
The Queen's University of Belfast
University Road, Belfast

ISBN 0 85389 413 2

Printed by W. & G. Baird Ltd, Antrim

CONTENTS

PREFACE

This book contains the proceedings of a conference held at the Marine Hotel, Dun Laoghaire (27–28 September 1991). 'Culture in Ireland: Division or Diversity?' was organised by the Cultures of Ireland Group, whose patron is Mary Robinson, President of the Irish Republic. The Cultures of Ireland Group (their names are listed below) convened as the result of an initiative from Constance Short, cultural adviser to Co-Operation North. Co-Operation North generously facilitated a series of meetings and soundings among a wide range of people, South and North, who are interested in Irish cultural questions.

The conference programme stated:

> The difficulties Irish politicians, North and South, have experienced in seeking agreement on new structures, have focussed attention on the cultural roots of our problems. Both Nationalists and Unionists use cultural arguments to validate ideologies which can be narrow, exclusive and productive of violence. Dissatisfaction with this situation has generated much debate during the last twenty years. Three cultural conferences in Northern Ireland in the past three years – 'Varieties of Irishness', 'Varieties of Britishness' and 'All Europeans Now?' – have led to government initiatives in the spheres of education, community relations and local government. These include, for example, a syllabus for all schools which involves 'Education for Mutual Understanding' and 'Cultural Heritage'. The aim of this conference is to start a process which will initiate a similar programme of cultural action in the Republic of Ireland.

The Cultures of Ireland Group sought the participation of academics, writers, educationalists, clergy, journalists, people active in community ventures and in the arts, as well as members of every political party and every major cultural body throughout Ireland. Although there were a few gaps in the attendance, and no single gathering can claim to be representative, the issues were discussed with breadth, depth and the shock of new insights.

These issues came up under the three broad headings: Irish Ireland, British Ireland and Religious Ireland – categories which the conference examined in both their historical and contemporary aspects. Such ground-clearing turned out to be an essential prelude to ideas about the necessity for new categories and 'new language'. Mr Chris Flood TD, Minister of State at the Department of Health, whom we were very pleased to welcome to the conference, also stressed 'talking to, and listening to, each other' and 'a process of dialogue' as contributing to 'our acceptance of cultural diversity'. We are grateful for permission to include his speech in this book.

The conference's two terms, 'Division or Diversity?' derive from a disagreement between historians. The late F. S. L. Lyons (in *Culture and Anarchy in Ireland*, 1979) thought that cultural differences in Ireland made political division inevitable. Roy Foster, in his lecture 'Varieties of Irishness', delivered at the first Northern cultural conference, argued against the 'bleak pessimism' of Lyons's view that Irish cultural diversity after 1900 'was inevitably confrontational'.

We hope that this conference has advanced the argument – and not, ultimately, in the direction of pessimism. There is still a vast amount to be done and overcome in Northern Ireland. But I think it emerged that cultural self-analysis within the Republic, and consequent action, can help the process in the North, besides being desirable for internal reasons.

The conference-proceedings, like those of the Northern conferences (also published by the Institute of Irish Studies), consist of prepared papers, workshop reports and spontaneous discussion from the floor. Occasionally I have had to credit a comment simply to 'Voice', when somebody failed to say their name into the microphone. But the whole conference, indeed, amounted to a succession of voices – concerned, informed, urgent.

Edna Longley, for Cultures of Ireland Group:
Niall Crowley (Hon. Chairperson), *Andy Pollak* (Chairperson), *Constance Short* (Administrator), *Barbara Sweetman FitzGerald, Fergus O'Ferrall, Mary Holland, Joseph Liechty, Edna Longley, Terence Brown, Raymond Gillespie.*

PART I

KEYNOTE ADDRESSES AND DISCUSSION

Hon. Chairman's Introduction

Niall Crowley

Your Excellency, Ladies and Gentlemen. I would like first of all to welcome you all here this evening to what promises to be a very exciting experience for all of us – and a worthwhile experience, and hopefully one that will be the start of something in terms of the cultural life of this island of ours, and indeed in many other facets of the life of this island. My job is to introduce briefly the President, who needs no introduction from me.

But Mary Robinson, both as President and as Mary Robinson, has been a great champion of the rights of all the peoples living in this island – their right to live in peace, harmony and with dignity and respecting each other's beliefs, respecting each other's traditions. She is, introduction required or not, an appreciated guest here today – President, it is a special privilege and a real pleasure for all of us that you have agreed to open this conference – it's an endorsement and a dimension that is very important to us.

Co-Operation North, as you probably know, sponsored the formation of this group: The Cultures of Ireland Group. The group was set up to explore in a logical way the diversity of traditions in the island of Ireland, and through that exploration we hope to arrive at practical ways of implementing programmes which will encourage and get the various communities to respect one another, and respect one another through their diverse traditions.

And even if Mary Robinson had never become President, perish the thought, she would through her beliefs and her commitment have been the obvious choice as the patron of such a cause. And now happily she is here today as our President, and can add the great prestige of her position as head of state to this cause and to this conference. In our groups we will concentrate on the work and attitudes in the Republic, as the work in Northern Ireland has been carried on in a quite wonderful way by the Central Community Relations Unit at Stormont and the Community Relations Council of Northern Ireland. And, of course, we hope to work together and complement one another in an informal way as we have already been doing in the build-up to this conference. We want cultural traditions to become shared experiences, whatever the traditions and beliefs. President – thank-you for being here, which has given our work an extra dynamic and extra dimension of energy and enthusiasm, and thank-you even more for agreeing to open this conference. I know how much intelligent thought and commitment you put into preparing for such occasions. And that is already a happy and important hallmark of your Presidency. We therefore look forward with considerable anticipation to what you have to say to us today.

MARY ROBINSON

An tUachtarán

A Cháirde,

I was delighted, last April, when Constance Short wrote to invite me to open today's conference. I had no hesitation in accepting and I am glad to be here with you now.

The overall theme you have for your discussions, 'Culture in Ireland: Division or Diversity?', is a challenging one. I will not attempt to answer the question but I would like to set out a few thoughts on the subject.

It is, I believe, correct to recognise the variety of cultural traditions and experience which exists in Ireland. It is also profoundly important that we should confront these individual traditions and study the relationship in which they stand to each other and the meaning which each has for the other.

The ideal should be a synthesis between our various traditions, a reconciliation between different heritages and values. It is, I think, possible to conceive of a single Irish cultural identity which would embrace a diversity of influences. As Hubert Butler – to whose example this conference is dedicated – has himself said:

> It is as neighbours, full of ineradicable prejudices, that we must love each other, not as fortuitously 'separated brethren'.

It is, of course, extremely difficult to reach a satisfactory definition of culture. It may be understood, perhaps, as that state of intellectual and artistic development which results from our interaction with our environment, our climate, our past and all the many economic and social factors, internal and external, which affect our lives.

Not unnaturally, the results of this process can vary from one community to another, even on an island as small as ours. But there are, I believe, certain fundamental characteristics which form part of the cultural inheritance of all Irish men and women. Certain habits of mind and means of expression have, over the centuries, generated a distinctively Irish vision of the world. There is an attachment to the ancient traditions and civilisation of this island which has survived all political divisions. W.B. Yeats was, perhaps, thinking of this original cultural unity of the Irish when he asked the question: 'Have not all nations had their first unity from a mythology that marries them to rock and hill'?

One notices throughout Ireland a keen preoccupation with the Irish identity, with what it means to be Irish. This has its roots in our turbulent past and in the continuing divisions of the present day. It also stems, however, from the rapid social and economic changes experienced by most Western countries in recent times and from the readjustments dictated by our deepening involvement with our European neighbours. There is a growing recognition that we are living in a world whose contours are changing with breath-taking speed and in which the safe certainties of the past are constantly being challenged.

Our identity must be constantly rediscovered, or re-created, if we are to come to terms with these changing circumstances. We must keep open that swinging door, that concept of the Fifth Province.

Within our island, there is a growing acknowledgement of diversity and of the legitimacy of the various traditions. We have long left behind what Tim Pat Coogan calls 'the great simplicities of the turn-of-the-century Gaelic Renaissance'. There remains, however, considerable scope for suspicion and misunderstanding. There remains much to divide us. I hope that, in time, the divisions which still afflict us today will yield to a new order based on profound respect for diversity and for the rights and aspirations of others.

I would like to see both traditions working towards this goal by coming to accept each other's different inheritances and by recognising the legitimacy of each other's values and beliefs.

Organisations such as yours have an important role to play in this process. The cross-fertilisation of ideas between our various traditions is essential to the development of mutual understanding and 'Cultures of Ireland' is making a significant contribution to this work.

At national and at local level, we must exploit cultural diversity as a potential asset under, rather than as a source of, tension or conflict.

A practical example of this is Annaghmakerrig in New Bliss, Co. Monaghan, a house bequeathed by Hubert Butler's brother-in-law, Tyrone Guthrie, to the nation for use as a retreat by artists, writers and musicians from all parts of this island. Like Butler, Guthrie had been educated in England, but chose to return to live in Ireland. He made Annaghmakerrig his family home from 1956 until his death in 1971.

The location of Annaghmakerrig, close to the border, is also significant in terms of the dualism that is so often present in our Irish cultural identity and so reflected in our art and literature. It is what Richard Kearney (in *The Irish Mind*) calls 'this Joycean counterpointing of the foreign and the familiar'. Kearney goes on to describe Seamus Heaney as:

> A Northern Irish poet who migrated South, at once exiled and at home, haunted by borders and partitions, exposed to the culture of coloniser and colonised, Catholic and Protestant, Gael and Saxon [who] has also practised an art of making contradictions dance.

All of our poets – whether Yeats or Kavanagh, Heaney or Mahon or MacNeice – illustrate these various contradictions and make similar pleas for the validity of a double cultural residence.

It is perhaps here, in this concept of a double cultural residence, a kind of Annaghmakerrig of the heart and mind, a fifth province, that we could, as a people, find our true identity, embracing all traditions and denying none, a new self-awareness which accepts the diversity of our various cultures but, within this diversity, finds unity. Thank you.

Conference Chairman's Introduction

Patrick MacEntee S.C.Q.C.

Ladies and gentlemen. It is now my pleasant duty and honour to take over the chairmanship of this conference, which has been opened with such élan by her Excellency the President's stimulating and thought-provoking speech.

I am deeply honoured to be asked to chair this conference and feel remarkably ill-equipped for the task. With such a distinguished gathering I am very conscious that a mere barrister is liable to get himself into deep water.

I am not, however, totally without qualification. I was reared in the town of Monaghan during the war years – the child of an Irish father and an English mother – and an English mother who was extremely proud of her Englishness. In a town where many schoolboys were not conspicuously pro-British, I learned from a very early age that diversity and division are realities of life. But, as Jacques Darras said at a previous conference – 'Everyone has to live with his frontiers and I myself would rather live astride them'. I, too, would rather live astride our diversities and to an extent I do. It's not the most comfortable of places, but I think in the long run it's the most rewarding.

We are setting about a heavy task and I would hope that we might focus on positive things, and that we would come away from this conference having had a frank, open discussion leading to concrete proposals for the future. I would hope that we would arrive at concrete proposals about the future of this group and where it might go from here. We would hope that at the end of our conference we would have a firmer and more rounded view as to what we wish to say to opinion formers, to government, to the Department of Education and to the media about re-examining curricula, about programme making on radio and television, about the entire area of the arts. Our purpose, as I see it, is to achieve clarity of vision about cultural diversity and divisions so that in the future cultural diversity can become a source of enrichment to all who live on this island rather than a cause of the violence which has been endemic in our societies, North and South, for too long. The task we set ourselves is not an easy one, and we can't expect to get any high degree of agreement upon it. None the less, we must try, because the present bloodshed and destruction are intolerable.

Your programme indicates that this conference, as is appropriate for any cultural group in the south of Ireland, has a patron saint. It is most appropriate that our patron saint should be Hubert Butler. He has written: 'Living in social harmony is a very difficult art – the most absolute concentration is required and the most perfect equilibrium. Our island is dangerously tilted towards England and towards Rome, good places in themselves, but best seen on the level'. Hubert Butler was a man of vast humanity and great humour and it is an indication of his appropriateness for the office of patron saint of this conference that he could see humour and value even in bad hagiography. (See 'Saints, Scholars and Civil Servants' in *The Children of Drancy*, Lilliput Press, 1988).

Ladies and gentlemen, I think at the outset it might be no harm if I indicated in the most general terms what I take to be a general broad definition of culture, and I would, for the purpose of this conference, define culture in its widest sense, as including the ideas and learned behaviour which go to make up peoples' ways of life. Four broad categories come to mind. (1) How people react to their environment – how they work, build, feed and clothe themselves: how they group themselves together and choose their allies and by implication, how they exclude others from their group. (2) How they express and educate themselves. (3) How they enjoy themselves – how they express themselves in the arts and play. (4) How they deal with the great metaphysical problems – life, death, God and thus how they worship. That, in general terms and for the purpose of this conference is how I understand it.

In my friend Frank Callinan's edition of *Parnell, a memoir* by Edward Byrne, there is a quotation from Parnell: 'A big man requires a big horse to ride – not two small horses'. I have thought about this, and I suggest that a big man requires a big horse and a small horse and perhaps a number of horses, not to mention perhaps donkeys and jennets and mules for the long haul. It is diversity, it is choice, it is the excitement of getting our cultures into good order that is life-enhancing. From a position of equality and strength, from a position of confidence, our several cultures can act upon each other to enrich all our lives.

This evening we will have two speakers. Jennifer Johnston is one of Ireland's most distinguished novelists. She is a member of a distinguished literary and theatrical family. I had the honour to dine with her father on two occasions. When he came to Dublin he used to dine at the King's Inns, and it was a great honour to be invited to dine with him. A most humorous and delightful and erudite man he was indeed. The first time I dined with him I had very little to say for myself but to my surprise, I was invited again. On the second occasion I had rather more to say and was not invited a third time. Jennifer's mother, Sheila Richards, was a great lady of the Irish theatre and television and a person of great warmth and generosity. Jennifer was born in Dublin, and now lives in Derry. She is the author of many novels, *How Many Miles to Babylon?*, *The Old Jest,* and most recently, *The Invisible Worm,* which has received wide critical acclaim. She is remarkably well equipped both by history and experience to contribute to your proceedings and it is a deep honour and privilege to introduce Jennifer Johnston.

The next keynote address will be given by Brendan Kennelly. Brendan is a poet, a Kerry-born poet, he is a Professor of English at Trinity College, Dublin, and perhaps his best known work is *Cromwell* – a highly unorthodox exploration of Irishness and Britishness. A new epic work called *The Book of Judas* is about to be published and I'm honoured to call upon him to deliver the second keynote address.

JENNIFER JOHNSTON

This is my home and country. Later on
perhaps I'll find this nation is my own;
but here and now it is enough to love
this faulted ledge, this map of cloud above,
and the great sea that beats against the west
to swamp the sun.

John Hewitt speaks in those lines for a substantial number of
people whose home is on this island; many people who would
themselves be unable to put the finger on the spot with such stern
honesty.

I looked up the word nation in the O.E.D. I thought I knew the
meaning, but I had to be sure: 'A distinct race or people, characterised by common descent, language or history, usually organised
as a separate political state and occupying a definite territory.' And
then below: 'The Nation. The whole people of a country.' It is not
yet time to write Robert Emmet's epitaph, and I have never been
able to work out why my father, Denis Johnston, suggested that it
was.

I am neither a philosopher nor a politician, an academic nor a
former of opinion in any way. All I know how to do is tell stories:
the same story, some people say, over and over again. That may be
true, but for me it has been something else, it has been a reassem-
bling of facts, my facts and an attempt to give those facts a relevance, to make me relevant, to identify myself: not give myself a
label, because we are all diminished by labels, but to shout that I
am on the side of the nation, with a small n, while recognising that,
for all our fine words, we have not yet achieved the Nation with a
large one.

Here I present you with some of the facts, and perhaps, but I
hope not, a little bit of fiction.

I was born in 1930; seven months after my father's first play, *The Old Lady Says No*, opened in the new and exciting Gate Theatre, and fifteen months before *The Moon in the Yellow River* opened in the Abbey. It was a time when the guardians of the staggering infant state were beginning to protect it, not only from its own dangerous thoughts, but also from malign influences from outside the island. There were, however, a number of people who wanted to explore the dangers of the world outside, to possibly Rock the Boat (a good old Protestant expression used in the twenties and thirties: don't rock the boat, keep your head down, button your lip), young people who wanted in their own way to be allowed to test the boundaries of our new freedom. Both my parents came into that category.

My father came from the privileged middle class: a big red brick house in Lansdowne Road with granite steps up to the front door and a tennis court in the back garden. His father was a judge, and indeed was elevated to the Supreme Court a couple of years before his death. He and my grandmother moved in legal and political circles, his friends were called Cosgrave, Costello, Biggar and McGilligan. He was a kind man, with sparkling blue eyes and a Northern voice. He drank a glass of Kruschen Salts every morning before shaving, he had a passion for trains, took the waters once a year in a place in Wales called Llandindrod Wells, and spent a holiday every year just outside Portrush, enjoying what he called the bracing air. He had arrived in Dublin towards the end of the last century, from Magherafelt in Co. Derry *via* the Malone Road, where his father, a successful tea merchant, had built himself a house.

At one stage in his life he had enthusiastically involved himself in politics. I quote here from an appreciation of the Judge written shortly after his death by a district justice called Louis. J. Walshe (in the *Irish Independent*): 'When I was a little lad, I remember one day standing on Magherafelt Square at a Home Rule meeting and joining in the cheers of the crowd, with all a boy's enthusiasm, at the fighting speech of a young Protestant barrister whose family had broken away from the narrow prejudices of their own people in Ulster to throw in their lot with Irish Nationalism. "Boys a boys, that's great spakin! Who is he at all?" cried a wildly excited old man beside me. 'That's James Johnston's . . . the tay man's son. He's after being made a councillor.' Only those who know Ulster can understand what it meant for a Protestant to declare himself in favour of self-government for Ireland. Only strong men were proof against the cruel boycotting and social ostracism that were used against them.

He was a loyal and committed Presbyterian and every Sunday he and my grandmother attended Adelaide Road Presbyterian Church. When he died in the early years of the war, as a Supreme Court Judge, he asked that his funeral be totally private, in fact only my father and his cousin Leo from Newry were present. We believe, though this may be fiction creeping in, that this demand of his was to save his many colleagues and friends the embarrassment of having to decide whether to honour the life of a distinguished Irishman or obey the Church who at the time did not allow Catholics to enter Protestant Churches or participate in Protestant ceremonies. A case, perhaps, of Don't Rock the Boat.

My father was educated at St Andrew's College and then sent to boarding school in Scotland; subsequently he went to Christ's College Cambridge and Harvard Law School. A distinguished surgeon and traveller called James Johnston Abraham wrote in his autobiography:

> Denis was a small boy in Dublin when I was an undergrad. It was the ambition of his father, Mr Justice Johnston that he should follow him in the law, and he was accordingly called to both the Irish and the English Bar. But he did not love the law enough. I remember one luncheon party at the old Grand Hotel in Trafalgar Square, when his father and I tried hard to make him stick to it. His father had visions of him becoming another Edward Carson, but he refused. He said he wanted to be a writer. I felt with his father at the time that he was making a mistake: writing is such a chancy job.

My grandparents were comfortable, gentle and most honourable people: they certainly feared God and probably honoured the King, though I wouldn't know about that. My father was their only child on whom they laid all their love and aspirations.

My mother's family was another kettle of fish. My grandfather, Johnny Richards, was also, like my father an only child, with some fairly well hidden scandal attached to his own father who ran away with his Colonel's wife and was never heard of again, leaving his rich and well connected wife and son in a house in Lower Fitzwilliam Street that had belonged to her family since it was built. I gather she was a somewhat sour old lady and I think he must have been a lonely child. He became a barrister, but went into the solicitors firm belonging to his mother's family. He married a young and beautiful girl from a large, impoverished but immensely cheerful family called Roper and over seventeen years they had five children. My mother was the youngest and, as both of her older sisters married young and had children, there must always seem to have been young people in the house and in the overflow house in Greystones, where weekends and summer holidays were spent.

My grandmother became a suffragette, until it was pointed out to her by Johnny that chaining herself to the railings in Stephen's Green would not be received kindly by his somewhat old-fashioned clients. He, himself, was an old-fashioned man, dragged into the twentieth century by his clatter of children; none of whom he would have considered turned out the way he might have wished, but he learned to put up with that. Juliet, his eldest daughter married a barrister, who, according to my father only got one brief, which he left on a Dalkey tram. He then himself left for Canada, bringing my aunt with him, but she hated it so much that she eventually returned to Dublin with two small children and lived with her parents until they died. She was a strong and wilful woman whom I loved deeply. After my grandmother died she lived in Greystones and her house became a second home for nephews and nieces and grandchildren. She played golf and bridge and went to the races and during the war ran the St John's Ambulance Brigade in Wicklow. Her only son was in the Royal Marines.

She seemed untroubled by the existence or non-existence of God; in fact I remember her shouting at me once: 'There's only one prayer worth knowing: From ghoulies and ghosties and long leggedy beasties and things that go bump in the night dear Lord deliver us.' I never knew whether to laugh or take her seriously. One Sunday morning during the war, she banged a hat on to her head and marched me off to the Church, where she joined with great gusto in the service. She had just heard the news that Tony's ship, the Barham, had been sunk off Cape Town, and had obviously decided that her one prayer was inadequate to deal with the situation. Tony survived the war. The next daughter, Brownie, married a young Catholic barrister. This didn't in any way upset my grandparents except for the fact that the marriage ceremony had to take place in Holyhead, as no Catholic priest in Dublin would marry them.

'Infernal rubbish' was Johnny's comment. The eldest son of the family, Billy, a young lawyer, just starting in the family firm, was killed at Suvla Bay, where so many of the Dublin Fusiliers were slaughtered, on 15th August 1915.

This is part of a letter written to Johnny, dated 10 August 1915:

Dear father,
We have been fighting now for four days and I am sorry to say have lost most of the battalion. We were doing fatigues for the first two days and only lost about ten men, but yesterday morning about 3a.m. we were called up to stop a counter attack. In about two hours we lost twelve officers and about four hundred and fifty men. How I got through I shall never understand, the shrapnel and bullets were coming down like hail. Three men were shot handing me messages. The colonel also got through all right. Luke had his hand blown off but is all right. Martin got a slight wound in his arm. In the last five nights I have had about five hours sleep but still feel fairly fit in body but my heart is broken for all those fellows I liked so much. I am at present watching the two divisions which are coming up to relieve us getting the most awful shelling. We are at present much nearer to the enemy than they are, but they are giving us a rest. When they come up we will all attack. After yesterday I have a feeling I will get through this job. I must shut up as I have a great deal to do before this show starts. Give my love to mother and everyone at home. I hope you are well. Thanks ever so much for all you have done for me.
Yours as ever Billy

My grandmother was deeply affected by his death. She also lost a brother in France.

Years after those three came my uncle Teddy and my mother. My mother was always known as the little yellow monkey. My uncle Teddy who was impressively handsome, married an English girl of whom his family did not totally approve, took to drink and died in his early thirties. Unlike the rest of her family my mother, the baby, was let be educated at home. She went with her great friend Pet Wilson, a Catholic, whose father was a Q.C. and a great friend of Johnny's, to Alexandra School; a school that had been started by an enlightened feminist and educationalist with the idea that it was time that girls would be given as good an education as their brothers: the world could also belong to woman. There she was taught history by Dorothy MacArdle and began to act in school plays; she was not afraid of anything except the dark. She was in a way more privileged than her older sisters in that her faculties were expanding and her sensibilities were sharpening in an amazingly changing world.

Old snapshots show picnics, tennis parties, fancydress dances, hunting, sailing, theatrical productions mounted in the garden, crowds of cheerful young people in cars, on bicycles: the sun always seemed to be shining. The Easter Rising had happened three years before and the war against the British was going on all around; none of them really ever spoke about it in later years, it was almost as if it were something that had nothing to do with them. It all happened in another country.

My mother made up her mind to be an actress. She began to act and then to direct plays with the Drama League, and then after a while she began to work in the Abbey Theatre, under an assumed name, because of possible paternal disapproval. The gaff was blown one day by a friend of Johnny's in the Kildare Street Club, who congratulated him on the girl's talent and he stamped home to read the riot act, but his children could wheedle anything out of him and he became resigned to the fact that the infernal girl was on the stage, and she assumed her own name once more.

My mother never took to my father's parents. Like so many people in the South, she despised the Northerners, she made jokes about their accents, their worthiness, their air of successful common sense, their fine Victorian house with its tasselled blinds, potted plants and dignified furniture. They tolerated her, but only just, and I don't think that my Johnston grandparents and my Richards grandparents enjoyed much mutual social life.

My brother and I were protected from the vagaries and vicissitudes of our parents' relationship by two remarkable women. The first was our nanny – Nono as she was called for pretty obvious reasons – who came to us not long after I was born and stayed until my brother went to school, about nine years or so, I suppose. She was Church of Ireland, orderly, firm but never either unfair or unkind. She had a sense of humour and handled chaos admirably. She taught me to be good. I didn't necessarily stay good, but I always remained aware of the power of goodness.

May Cunningham was a Dublin woman, several years older than my mother. She arrived to work for my parents when they were

married and brought with her a network of friends and family –
always someone to fill a gap, always someone to deal with a crisis.
Between them all they seemed to own Dublin; seemed, in fact, to
have owned it for centuries. They knew everyone, their histories,
their tragedies, their comedies, both high – the quality as May called
them – and low. May was, and indeed I'm glad to say still is, a devoted
Catholic; she produced Papal flags for us to hang out of our
windows on suitable occasions and saw that we all had poppies on
Remembrance Day. She had a passionate love for us all. She knew
where she wanted us to go, and how she wanted us to be. She never
deviated from her desire to see us, to use her words, 'well rared'.

May had politics, which none of my immediate family seemed to
me to have. She had history. She had stories about a turbulent
Dublin that my parents pretended never existed. She had a sister
with wild red hair who worked in Cassidy's in Wicklow Street and
once a week put on some splendid green uniform with a cocked
hat and went off to do something mysterious. I asked May in later
years if it had been Cumann na mBan. 'Certainly not,' she an-
swered with scorn. She believed in God, which seemed more than
any of my family, even the Catholics, seemed to do. They all had a
certain laxity about their obligations and from time to time made
fierce and, to a child dangerous, jokes about God. My mother
always said that the laxity on the part of the Catholic relatives was
because they had all been to school in England and English
Catholics saw things in a different way to Irish ones. May lit candles
in Donnybrook Church when my mother lost things and they
became found. She had songs which she sang at the drop of a hat:
'We are the boys of the old Brigade' mixed with Moore's Melodies
and 'Rosemarie I love you'; 'I dreamed that I dwelt in marble halls'
and 'Tramp, tramp the boys are marching'. They compared pretty
favourably in my mind with my father's renderings of Gilbert and
Sullivan and his operatic arias with very funny words written by
himself.

I was supposed to be going to go to school in England. The war
saved me from that. I have never worked out why they had even
considered such a fate for me. When the war was over my brother
was packed off on the B and I boat three times a year, with a whole
army of other teenage boys to such places as Rugby, Eton,
Marlborough, Downside, Ampleforth. Saloon and Third they went
and we drove down to the end of the South Wall to wave them
goodbye. Saloon and Third. No one went First all the way, my

mother explained, only snobs and people with more money than sense.

I still have a crazy notion that it wasn't so much to do with the idea that we might come back better educated and therefore better prepared to deal with life, but with the way they wanted us to speak. To have an accent of any sort – my God they didn't want us to speak like English people – was some sort of treachery. My brother passed muster, but my mother was always convinced that I invented my voice in order to punish her for something.

The war locked us in on ourselves. The boundaries of freedom shrank. The island shrank in size. The war was beyond the border, a corner of the island was blacked out. We could only move as far as our bicycle legs would take us. There were no more holidays to my Johnston relations in England or even to cold Portrush. No more theatrical tours to London or America for my mother, no more Hugh Hunt and Tanya Moseivich at the Abbey, no more bananas, and no more father. Never.

In one way my own personal boundaries were extending. In the period of time when my brother was very small and needed Nono's entire attention I moved around with May. Her family and friends welcomed me into their homes. Her nephews, nieces, friends became very much part of my life. They came to tea with me and I with them, just as the children of my mother's friends came. One day I was visiting May's old aunt Essie. At the end of the cul de sac where she lived was a sweet factory and I was taken down to see it. I must have been about eight or nine. One of the women looked at May and said, 'God love her, you'ld know she wasn't one of us.' I still remember the words and the rounded door of the sweet factory and the puzzlement that I felt.

My mother only allowed the wireless to be used when she was at home . . . was it censorship, of which she stormily disapproved, or a feeling that some one might break the machine, the only reliable link with the world outside? A bit of both, I think. She had come in one day to find Mrs K., who did the hard scrubbing round the place, listening with enormous pleasure to Lord Haw Haw and then the ban was imposed. Mrs K. was an energetic and vocal hater of anything English. As she scrubbed she smoked non-stop and delivered magnificent diatribes against England and longed for its speedy defeat at the hands of the Germans. She had a great fighting spirit, something my mother always admired, and a great way with words. 'Any day now,' she told my mother once as we sat in the kitchen drinking cups of tea, 'that octopus Hitler will hold all of Europe in his testicles.' My mother shut her eyes, obviously picturing it. 'And that,' shouted Mrs K., 'will serve the fucking English right.'

As I grew from the nursery and the kitchen into some modest independence, the world in which my mother lived so actively became apparent to me. She had left the Abbey and had become a free-lance actress and director; and with a partner, a man, who for his own reasons which I don't know, had preferred to spend the war years in Ireland rather than England, had started a company of her own. They took a huge gamble and put on plays in the Olympia Theatre, which had in fact been a music hall theatre and was at what people said was the wrong end of Dame Street. They played Shaw, Shakespeare, Giraudoux, O'Casey and many other dramatists whose names I don't remember, to reasonably enthusiastic audiences, but it was with Paul Vincent Carroll's almost soap operas about the Glasgow blitz, *The Strings are False*, that they had a great success. The play ran for nine or ten months to packed houses, so greedy were people for even a vicarious view of what it was like to be at war. My mother decided to keep the theatre open for the first three days of Holy Week, something that had never been done before. The fury of the Church was turned on her. She was threatened by telephone and letter. Pickets were put on the theatre. Bomb threats were made and each evening before the performance the theatre had to be searched by the bomb squad before the crowds could be let in. The queue stretched right down Dame Street. The pickets and the angry priests at the doors stopped no-one going in. It was all quite frightening at the time and I remember longing for her to give in as I was sure she was going to be killed. A little battle, but definitely Rocking the Boat in its own way.

That's it really. A bit too anecdotal perhaps. They're all dead now, all those old people, except for May. I know where their graves are. Isn't that very nearly all we need to know when we think about home or nations?

BRENDAN KENNELLY

Ladies and gentlemen, I would like to speak if possible without judging, or passing what looks like final judgement on others. I fear this kind of judgement because it really means that one's ignorance masquerades as knowledge, so you turn on others the revealing spotlight you take care not to turn on yourself. But how is it possible to speak of Ireland without using language of judgement, and therefore of blame? Blame is useless – it's like revenge or cynicism. It probably does more damage to the person who lays it than to the person on whom it is laid. Irish conversation is riddled with the language of judgement and blame – there's a Russian proverb which I put into a poem: 'The devil is always blaming someone/ Bricks of blame pave the floor of hell/ The girls are cold, the horses lost in the mountains/ And truth lies bleeding at the bottom of the well'. These days Dublin is a city of scandals and blame. And how it loves it! A journalist said to me last Wednesday night: 'The city is full of scandals – Thanks be to Jesus – they're keeping me alive .' Anything at all to flog the dying horse of middle-aged male interest. I shall try to talk without judging or blaming, but as you see, I'm already finding it very difficult.

A few points to lead into what I want to say. I've a couple of favourite sentences which I never fail to marvel at. 'Before Abraham was I am' 'True progress is possible only between opposites': the disruption of chronology, the embrace of polarities – we have to talk in any such gathering of Catholic and Protestant. Ninety-five per cent Catholic, five per cent Protestant – St Stephen's day, Boxing Day, whatever about the Jews, Muslims, Hell's Angels, and atheists. What does this majority/minority thing do to peoples' minds? What does it feel like to be of the five per cent? Do Southern Protestants suffer a lot from Catholic assumptions? I would like to ask a few questions about Southern Catholicism. What interest, if any, has it got in ethics? Ethics means trying to be fair, fair-minded, responsible to the community. I want to talk about conscience. Stephen Dedalus says at the end of the *Portait of the Artist:* 'I go to encounter for the millionth time the reality of experience, and to forge in the smithy of my soul the uncreated conscience of my race'. I would like to suggest to you that Joyce's idea there is that Irish Catholicism was without a conscience. It still is. This consciencelessness is a very pervasive thing and all you have got to do is look at your self if you are one of the ninety-five per cent before, during and after Mass. Last year 4000, over 4000 Irish girls had abortions in England. But are we aware in conscience of this, and if we were what would we do? But we dump our young women and 4000 foetuses on the English. That is increasingly what the English are for us. A dump. While we practise our superior morality. I want to ask that question: to what extent are we using Britain as a place for dumping our problems? Last year I had a dramatic version of my attempt to understand history – *Cromwell* – produced in England. And every night I walked over a bridge to the theatre and every night I passed beggars sitting on the bridge, and I could tell by their faces that they were Irish, and I think they could tell from my walk that I was Irish as well. My face or my fatness or whatever it was. And on the third night a little girl looked up and said 'What are you doing here?' and I said 'I have a play on here', and she said 'Would you have a fiver?' and I gave her a few bob and she said 'That won't get me back will it' and I said 'It won't' and I looked at her and she was like a cardboard child – they have nothing and they are ignored. And if you talk to any of the Irish in London, any of the twenty thousand dumped on England, they feel literally dumped. We are great for shedding responsibility, and then dressing it up as something else. And that's what I mean by the Irish Catholic culture being still without a conscience in many respects. I could work it out in other ways as well.

Is it proper to ask this question: if we dump our young women with their problems on England, do we Irish men, we Irish middle-aged men and women, do we just say to our young women: 'Go to hell with your problem, don't bother me, I don't know you – I don't want to know you, I don't want to know about you'. I would like to suggest that too as a possible subject for discussion, that a lot of Irishmen hate women. Hence the jokes and the joviality and the dumping of women. A lot of Irishmen dump their women when they have got ten years out of them. Now, I would like to connect this sad reality of dumping with what I see as a necessity. The necessity is the feminisation of Irish life.

A lot of Irishmen would be less effeminate if they allowed their lives to be feminised. What is the word for this no-caring about women? I think it is called morality. It is also called respectability. Not as virulent a disease as it used to be, but still pretty virulent in Ireland , particularly in parts of Dublin. It strikes me at this stage that I am not talking about conscience at all, but about consciousness. I wonder what is the difference between them – is there any? If you were sufficiently conscious would you not have a discriminatory conscience? Who are the creators of consciousness in our society? Who stirs it? Who tries to raise it, shape it, direct it? Parents, teachers, writers, councillors. Do politicians work to raise it or suppress it? Or do they simply distort it and do they train themselves to distort it? Consciousness, I think, means the questing, vulnerable, promising, eager opening up of one's mind to the world of exciting alternatives. The sharpest consciousness never fully parts company with its opposite – unconsciousness. True progress is possible only between opposites. This is the flame in the dark – they need each other. But if there is no flame of sustained, developing consciousness, there is only the darkness of the closed mind. This is what I want to talk about, because I see it in myself, and I feel it in people about me.

What is this closed mind? And what are the sources of the bourgeois, middle-class refusal to concede even that it exists? It is rooted of course in history. The greater part of Ireland is the post-colonial end. But the effects of colonialism are still deeply buried and operative in the Irish psyche. In the South of Ireland there is still a mechanical undercurrent of dislike or hatred for the English. While in the North there is a prominent, predominant, unquestioning sense of loyalty to the Crown. But it is not a love of England that wins the loyalty of Ulster Unionists, it is fear and distrust of the Southern government and people. Attitudes of many people North and South are characteristic of the closed mind, which is marked by a fierce and automatic resistance to alternatives, and by an equally fierce assertion of its own limited but ferociously held viewpoints or beliefs. The closed mind over-simplifies reality in such a way that self doubt is as unthinkable as a deep tolerance of the rights of others. The closed mind leads to fanaticism. A fanatic is a terrorist who is himself terrified of alternatives. A fanatic is a person who can see only one point of view, and who sincerely believes that most other points of view are not merely wrong but have to be exterminated. Sometimes fanatics are very quiet, and enjoy prominent positions. A fanatic will always try to bend reality to his own design in different ways. He will work with unrelenting energy and dedication to achieve this. He is strong and sincere. He may well be incapable of insinceriy and he has an even more powerful weapon to aid him in his noble task – he has a closed mind, a truly terrifying weapon.

Until very recently both the Roman Catholic and the apologetic Church of Ireland – the 'button your lip' church – the chief Protestant church in the Republic – advocated and sustained the closed mind. But this is slowly changing – thanks, among other things, to the increasing independence of women. I think that in the old cliché of Mother Ireland – strangely enough – lies the answer to some of our problems. The sense of cultural difference and complexity introduced by a well-educated and independent minded generation of young women and men is also important here. There is also, above all, a sense that a church – any church – is not simply or solely composed of bishops and priests and nuns and various types of clerics. It is composed above all of people – ordinary members. The ordinary people of Ireland are speaking out against the IRA. The ordinary people of Ireland are also determined to show their church that they are no longer a subservient peasantry, but an independent, hardworking and civilised people, capable of making their own decisions about public and private matters. The ordinary people of Ireland can be quite extraordinary at times.

But evidence of the closed mind is everywhere. The closed mind, though firm and resolute in itself, is in fact terrified of expansion, especially of expression coming from strangers, oddballs and foreigners, wogs. Many of the Irish oddballs have been Irish writers who tried to understand and express their country and its people. The mark of any soul is its capacity for growth. God never created anything stagnant, anything that had not the potential for growth. It is sinful and criminal to restrict that potential, but that restriction is the function of the closed mind. In the North of Ireland people are murdering each other with skill and dedication, and predictable punctuality because they have closed minds. Catholic and Nationalist, Protestant and Unionist. Labels. Jennifer said labels are diminishing: Ireland is an island of labels. In that situation a man is not a man but a label, and he will kill on behalf of his particular label. When Shakespeare wrote *Macbeth* he believed a murderer must have pangs of conscience, but Shakespeare never came to Ireland or perhaps he never met the closed mind. If he did he turned his back on it and he was right. In Ireland you cannot turn your back on it.

Now it is a singular irony that women who were so long the victims of the closed mind, especially in marriage, but also all through society, have now become some of the most powerful critics of its effects and consequences. The fact that Ireland is at last opening up is due in considerable measure to these strong-minded women. This conference was largely organised by two women. I'm going to list a few women that I admire, women who are writing: Ann Hartigan, Katie O'Donovan, Paula Meehan, Eavan Boland, Rita Ann Higgins, Nuala Ni Dhomhnaill, Medbh McGuckian, Emma Cooke,and others. There's something happening, something happening. There's a special force in the writings of these women. I find it at times quite frightening, because they are dealing with feelings that were never talked about before. A few couple of years ago a male, about my own age, made an attack on Medbh McGuckian up at the Kavanagh week-end because he couldn't understand what she was saying. This made him very angry and he said: 'I don't know what you are saying and that means you are a bad poet'. That is a male way of saying it, so we almost have to learn a new language. In *Cromwell* I was saying that there is a Protestant language, and there is a Catholic language, and I really made an effort as a fairly typical Southern Irish Catholic country fella to understand Protestant language. I had the advantage of course of being educated, if that is the word, in Trinity, where I came in contact with Protestant ways of thinking and feeling . That is why I have come to believe that we should have two kinds of new churches, not Catholics and Protestants, but Cathestants and Protholics, who would mingle with each other. It's the sort of embracing of opposites that I hope we would see in the future, and I think the women are pointing the way in that direction. It's a very special personal and resonant force. It is typical of Jennifer this evening with her beautiful, humane and personal paper that she didn't have to go beyond men and women and those about her to find out the meaning of our situation. But a bloke begins to feel guilty unless he is dealing in some vast cosmic abstraction, so you will forgive me any parody that I make of philosophy. It is the kind of force that is crucial in the fight against the closed mind. This force is typical of the voices of victims who have become creators and critics. This force is

evident also in the work of women writers of a previous generation
who should be mentioned – people like Mary Lavin and Kate
O'Brien, who in more difficult and oppressive times fought the
good fight and wrote the good write against the closed mind.

What does one do with the closed mind? You try to open it up.
Businessmen, and lawyers, journalists, priests, civil servants, teachers, doctors and even academics, sportsmen and sportswomen and
their supporters, politicians, readers of newspapers, listeners to
radio, and viewers of television all have the opportunity, ability
and responsibility to lift the darkness from the heart and mind of
Ireland. I think the radio is one of the best ways. Women are
talking to people like Marion Finucane, Gay Byrne and Gerry
Ryan. Now a lot of fellas get very angry when women come on and
talk about problems that originally could have been mentioned
only in the confessional. I come from that generation. I was reared
on 'bad thoughts', if you know what I mean. I had to go to
confession and you said to the priest: 'I had bad thoughts – I saw a
breast, I looked and I saw two breasts. They were beautiful'. And
he said: 'Did you entertain the bad thoughts?' and I said, 'No
father, they entertained me'. They really made us incapable of
relationships – my generation. And I think that's true of a lot of
Catholic men of my age, of middle-aged men, and I look back now
at some of the youngsters growing up, and they are so committed
to 'yuppiedom' and money that it's not the 'bad thoughts' that are
going to cripple these fellas but the helpless commitment to an
idea of success. But males are victims, men are victims in Ireland of
things that they don't suspect at all.

Now it's impossible to understand Ireland without thinking
about England. They're physically close and politically bound up
with each other, but they have never until recently really spoken to
each other. They are speaking to each other now, leading politicians from both countries are trying to speak to each other, and I
think good will come from it. I have to say, I grew up in a country
village, and a lot of the fellas used to go to England and come back
at Christmas, and they would say: 'I made £30 a week. And they
would have a suit on them and a bit of an accent, and they would
buy drinks for everyone in the place, and then they would talk a bit
about sex, and everyone in the pub would be around , looking at
these emblems, these embodiments of freedom and opulence,
home for the Christmas holidays. And everybody couldn't wait to
get on the boat. England meant salvation, as only the oppressing

nation can. In its dealings with Ireland, however, it has often been insensitive, and heedless and unjust. Yet the worst thing about it is this unawareness. I tried to work it out in *Cromwell*: whereas the Irish problem is a small thing for the English, it is a very big thing for us. And what you have to try to get together in your mind is this problem of disproportion, this feeling that it is nothing, or very little for them, and a lot for us.

In our own turn of course, we have been murderous. Yet I believe, even in spite of that, the IRA or their representatives should be invited to speak to the Irish people on radio and television and the Irish people should be able to speak back. I'm saying now, and there is a consistent thing in what I am saying, progress is possible only between opposites. We must talk to our killers, our would-be killers. What we need is full honest communication, not murderous assassinations or cowardly bombs. Not to totally isolate subversives or terrorists. An imposed isolation strengthens the closed mind. In isolation it will simply justify its actions to itself more and more and glorify itself. With dialogue there is at least a hope of opening it up. Let the IRA speak in public to the people they are claiming to liberate, and let us discuss why and how and where this liberation is taking place, then we might begin to discover who is liberating whom. We will begin to find out what is really wanted. We will see who is really courageous and who is cowardly. Instead of killing each other, perhaps we can work towards a new tolerant Ireland where every voice is heard and respected and thought about. I'm not talking about some vague political Utopia, I'm talking about a small rainy island with lovely sunny moments somewhere in the Atlantic – an island that has not yet learned to be truly tolerant. A tiny island country that is full of promise because it is fertile and beautiful and has a lot of problems, and a lot of decent, hardworking intelligent people to solve these problems, and go on to shape one of the most attractive countries in the world. Also, England does not listen as it should. That is, in a spirit of goodwill and understanding. Or when it does listen, that act of compassionate listening is too brief.

Ireland is now a country for young men and young women. Not a country for old men – it never really was. Young people are beginning to sense their own power. Their minds are opening, but the situation is difficult. Many of them are unemployed. Unemployment is an insult to human dignity. Most people want to work

– most people deeply need to work. Unemployment is a chronic waste of energy and talent. It is also a source of cynicism, depression and despair. There is a great deal of that now in Ireland in the South. In the North too. There is more crime than ever before. A lot of crime is committed out of boredom. I teach occasionally in Mountjoy, and I know. Unemployment leads to crime. Boredom is generated by unemployment. It is very wrong. It is criminal of a government to allow unemployment to rise at the rate it is rising in Ireland at present. Yet, in spite of that, many Irish people are thinking and talking now in a fluent way about their country. They see that patriotism need not, should not, involve murder. They see that work and the dignity that goes with work are vital to true, visionary, practical patriotism. The best patriot is the best worker, and many young people in Ireland are simply ravenous for work. Attention must be paid to that fact – if attention is paid, crime will diminish, peace will be possible.

I won't go on about education. President Robinson mentioned Patrick Pearse. All I can say to you is Pearse has written one of the great essays on education. And it is not rhetorical – it is not couched in rhetoric. It is couched in a passionate love of justice. You look at education in Trinity or UCD, it is a bourgeois possession. There are no kids from Darndale or any of the invisible cities of Dublin passing through our universities, and the middle classes are passionately possessive of education. Nor should education be confined to the young. It should be available to people at their moment of need at whatever moment of their lives that occurs. This may happen at sixteen or sixty.

The Catholic Church is 2000 years old: it has still to grow up. It refuses women the right to become priests. The Catholic church is therefore rejecting one of its own most valuable sources of spiritual energy and passion. Throughout its history Ireland has always owed a very profound debt to its women, and it was rarely expressed. A church which refuses women the right to become priests is simply being perverse. Not recognising its own potential. It cannot see that it is gutting itself, cutting its own throat. Determined to remain stuck in a predictable spiritual rut 2000 years old, and refusing to grow up.

Growing up can be a very painful process. Sean O'Casey said that Ireland is the oldest civilisation in Europe but she is still in her teens. A teenage island old as the sea it squats in. Opening its eyes, stretching forth its hands. Growing up – sometimes I think Ireland is growing up against its own will, that it prefers to destroy itself, its fine people. Why can't the terrorists see that they aren't helping anyone to grow up, or are they committed to the non-growing of this country? There are people who are in love with stagnation. There's an element in all of us that is in love with stagnation. Are they determined to cripple and maim all growth? Is terrorism terrified of the potential in ordinary decent living for growth? Does it hate the promise in normality? Is it a fear, is it a dread of the normal? I think in Ireland we have to learn about this fluent, co-operative attitude of helping each other, helping our opposition both without and within. Catholic and Protestant, Jew, agnostic and atheist, Unionist, Nationalist, city people, country people, church and state, working together to produce a new Ireland. I hope this weekend some attempt will be made to define it – the Ireland that will emerge from trouble and darkness, from ignorance and prejudice , from tragedy and suspicion, from self-destruction and intolerance. Tolerance is a pleasant land – the journey towards it is arduous and challenging. It is the journey we have to make. Instead of killing we must create, instead of hating we must love, instead of sneering we must encourage. This may seem a romantic dream, it is not. It is a possibility. To achieve it we must get rid of our own closed minds for good and glory. We should have a kind of orgy this weekend. An orgy of perception. We must open up to each other, especially to what we sense is most different and difficult in each other. If we do this we will discover the truly hidden Ireland – not Corkery's romantic hidden one, but the island that has survived all kinds of violence, including violent parodies of itself. Not a sentimental Ireland, not a place to sing sloppy ballads or tell raucous yarns about, not a cynical, derisive and divisive island, but a keenly intelligent, humorous country, with people, who, knowing each other's creeds, beliefs and politics, are prepared in the decency of their hearts to tolerate each other, and above all to enjoy each other. That's not Utopia. That's Ireland. Or it can be if we work with the conscience and the consciousness that are, as I have tried to suggest this evening, when they are fluent and active, indistinguishable.

GENERAL DISCUSSION

Chairman:

After the contributions of Jennifer and Brendan one can only regret that we are not governed by creative artists, be they novelists or poets. Perhaps we should learn to think as creative artists. Imagine a poet in Aras an Uachtaráin, five novelists in the Supreme Court, a government of artists – but that is a pipe dream, and this evening and tomorrow we must seek to define where we are, where we want to go, and how we can hope to get there. Perhaps first of all we should consider *who* we are? We have had a wealth of stimulation from Jennifer and Brendan to help us towards an answer to this question. What do you think about this subject?

Desmond Fennell:

I would respond Mr Chairman, immediately, to your invitation to discuss the general course of the thing in the next few days. I have a serious reservation about the mental format which the programme imposes on the conference, and I think the best way to express it is to read a brief extract from a letter I sent to the Convenor, Constance Short.

I wrote: 'Let me explain briefly the lack of enthusiasm which caused me not to respond to your first letter' – this was to her second letter. 'Clearly the intention is to have a conference and debate on the present-day cultures of Ireland with some special regard to the Northern Ireland problem. This could be valuable, but for it to be actually valuable it would need to be really about the present-day cultures of Ireland, and your programme as set out does not promise that. It suggests that there are two main cultures in Ireland today and that these can be described as Irish-Ireland and British-Ireland. But the terms Irish-Ireland and Irish-Irelanders are dated to the early part of this century and there are hardly any people in Ireland today, to quote your programme, "describing themselves as Irish-Irelanders". Moreover, those in Ireland today who might be "so described by others", do not form a major segment, only a minority element of present-day Irish culture. This minority dissents from the general culture of Ireland today, which can be described as a variant of British culture with an American overlay. British in everything from language, "Auld Lang Syne", "For He's A Jolly Good Fellow" and the horse culture, to the legal system, parliamentary procedure, etiquette, much of television, and what hotels serve for breakfast. American in fast food, casual dress, television, business jargon and so on. The division within Northern Ireland is primarily not cultural but ethnic, a matter of national allegiance. So a conference on the actual cultures of Ireland today would, while taking account of what you call Irish Ireland culture, be mainly concerned with the regional and class variants of our Americanised British culture from Antrim to Kerry, and Mayo to Dublin. That would be dealing with the real Ireland that we inhabit and would therefore be of real value.' I'm afraid that the conference, as projected, will flail around in rhetorical abstractions and rehash old arguments that have little to do with the cultural realities of Ireland today.

Chairman:
Thank you for that interesting contribution. I am confident that when you have heard the contributions of Gearóid O'Tuathaigh, Terence Brown, Thomas Kilroy and David Stevens tomorrow, you will be quite happy that the format of the conference will be to your liking. And I hope that you will stay with us in that expectation.

Mary Henry:
I am a medical doctor. I responded immediately to the invitation to this conference. I was most enthusiastic about coming. I thought, perhaps, we were going to do something about the culture of the South. I identified a lot with what both Jennifer and Brendan have said – particularly about closed minds and dumping our problems onto Britain. If one criticises any part of our culture here I have found there is often more interest in finding a reason why one is a critic, rather than in looking at the situation being criticised. It is more comfortable if the critic can be dismissed as not truly Irish.

During the first referendum here, the so-called 'abortion referendum' (our first neverendum campaign as my children call it),

while speaking against the constitutional amendment at various
venues around the country I was constantly thought to be a Southern Irish Catholic. Being considered one of the ninety-five per
cent gave one tremendous strength in criticising our culture. But
very few people from the ninety-five per cent – they're probably all
here tonight – are prepared to criticise our culture here: very few
are prepared to say, as Brendan did, that we use Britain as a
dumping ground for our problems. I would like us to address this
lack of criticism of our culture by *all* of us who consider ourselves
Irish down here. Certainly I am Irish – no-one in my family even
went to work in England – they are all in Co. Cork. And I find this
lack of an English connection a constant disappointment to people, if I make any critical comments. Critics are easily dismissed as
having 'German mothers', or some other disqualification which
excludes them from 'pure Irishness'.

Brian Walker:
I am from Queen's University, Belfast. I'm a historian. Several of our
speakers have mentioned the importance of the past, and I'd like to
make a comment about that. I think we should be aware that our
understanding of the past is very often coloured by the contemporary world we live in. Frequently it shapes the way we remember the
past. Can I show this in two ways? One is in the Loyalist tradition. As
you are all no doubt aware, in the Loyalist tradition the battle of the
Boyne, the massacres of 1641, and the siege of Derry are very
important. And yet one hundred years after these events very few
people remembered them. Look at the *Belfast News Letter* two
hundred years ago, one hundred years after the Boyne. The Boyne
is not celebrated in a significant way. The massacres of 1641 were
largely forgotten because most of the survivors left and very few
people in Ulster today can claim ancestry going back that long. The
Siege of Derry was celebrated in the late eighteenth century by an
annual walk around the walls with both Catholic and Protestant
clergy. Then of course this all changed, and it changed because in
the late nineteenth century with a new Unionist movement emerging, people wanted to construct a history that fitted in with their
current needs, so these events were remembered and other events
such as the United Irishmen were very conveniently forgotten.

And I would put it to you that this is also true on the Nationalist
Catholic side. An argument has been put forward today by a
number of speakers talking about a colonial past. But this very

much fits in with the post 1916 separatist ideas that emerged in twentieth-century Ireland. Because if we look at Ireland before that, this is not necessarily an argument that would be held by everyone. Ireland in the nineteenth century was not a colony – it was a fully integrated part of the UK, it sent MPs to Westminster, and Ireland in the eighteenth century was not a colony like the American colonies were – it was a kingdom under the British crown. It was not a colony. But of course, post 1916, people wished to construct a history that fitted in with their contemporary needs, so they looked at it in this way. This is not of course to say that there weren't tremendous problems in the relationship between Ireland and England. But we can sometimes put these matters under a simplistic label like 'colonial' whereas a particular circumstance may not be colonial at all when considered in its context.

So I would say that we do have to be very careful when we are viewing history. We need to take care that we don't allow it to be shaped by needs after the event. We have to be careful that our perceptions are not shaped simply by what happened in the twentieth century.

Chairman:
With that warning in mind, Professor Clare?

Anthony Clare:
I'm a psychiatrist and I felt moved to reply to Mary Henry. I don't know whether it has any bearing on the culture of Ireland, division or diversity, but it is something which I personally have felt like getting off my chest since I've come back here three years ago after twenty years across the water. It is a curious paradox that Mary can say, and there isn't a collective groan of disbelief, that we cannot criticise ourselves. Because I think we rarely do anything else. But at the same time she is articulating a truth. And that is: that we cannot bear to be criticised. And so we do both. It seems to me that the way it can be partially looked at is certainly through the eyes of my own field: that, in a sense, each of us is a patient by being Irish. We are maimed. And as we look at our past we have one of two choices. In making sense of it we have in the end to fall in love with it. We have to actually love ourselves as Irish, and I don't think we do. I think running through many of us is a profound self-disgust. Sometimes it is very apparent, and people I think engage in an orgy of self-destruction which in one sense – our violence – can be

seen. But sometimes it is much more covert. It only appears when we are criticised, and then we respond with great venom and vehemence because the criticism touches on a profound doubt inside ourselves. I know I'm talking personally, because I was born and reared in this country, through some of the things that Brendan talked about. I was an educated member of a middle class, voracious for hanging on to power. I was born into a family very split about its sense of itself as Irish, with a mother very profoundly anti-anything that was Gaelic and with a terrible envy for anything that was British. It certainly wasn't until I went personally to Britain and started to explore my own Irishness, that I saw so much of my anger, so much of my criticism of things Irish, was actually motivated by a profound dislike of many aspects of being Irish.

I had a single choice and that is you somehow come to terms. You pull together that which is Irish as a fact, as a reality, in the same way that any other nation will do it with their own essence. But we have profound difficulties in doing it, for reasons which I hope will come up in the next day and a half.

But one of the ways, it seems to me, that one might begin to proceed, is what one would encourage a patient to do, and that is what Jennifer did, I understand. I was late, but I asked everybody: 'What did Jennifer Johnston say?' and they all said the same thing: Jennifer (which is very reassuring, and somewhat rare on occasions in Irish settings), they all said you talked about yourself. Now the interesting thing about us Irish is we *think* we do that all the time. But we don't, you know, anything near as much as you think. We are masters of evasion with the English language. We use it to keep people away as much as to reveal. In fact, I think we conceal continually with language, which is one of the reasons we produce such first-class poets. Amongst the hopes I have in coming here, is to hear people talking about themselves personally: about what has made them – the influences, British/Irish/Gaelic/non-Gaelic, I don't care, Catholic/Protestant – but not talking in terms of those institutions out there. If I hear any more talk about referenda, Catholic Church, IRA, Ulster Unionist, I certainly won't stay a day and a half. I want to hear people come clean and say what they see as their essential Irishness, and how they feel. And I don't want to hear it as a fixture either, I'd like to hear it as a dynamic. That's to say, there's a struggle going on in each of us and we are uneasy about it. Of course, in other words, what I want is for each of you to turn yourselves into my patients. But then, those of you who know me ever so slightly know that I suffer from the most overweening form of grandiosity. But that I would identify as one of the elements of us Irish.

Chairman:
Now, Dr Clare, tell us why you suffer from a deep self-disgust.

Anthony Clare:
Because, in short, many of the things I am, I have been taught to dislike.

Chairman:
Name them.

Anthony Clare:
Catholic, lapsed, middle-class, non-Gaelic speaking. Incidentally, all the opposites of these things are hated too. We have our problems, in other words. That is a lot to be getting on with. You called it an orgy, I think, Brendan.

Chairman:
An orgy of perception.

Anthony Clare:
Precisely, and the invitation is that, and the perception that really needs to be exposed is our own. How we see ourselves. I don't want this to be exaggerated. I don't know what kind of coverage this is going to get, but 'Shrink exposes himself as a victim of self-disgust' is not a headline I look forward to. There are, in fact, many things that I can live happily with. And I have to say, one of the things for which I am very grateful to twenty years in Britain, was that Britain enabled me (as I suspect it has enabled many Irish people), to come to terms with myself as Irish. Britain can enable Irish people to live more happily with themselves as Irish, prouder of themselves as Irish. As it turned out in my case, I couldn't wait in the end to get back to this place, to live here as Irish. Because in the end, despite all the scandals, the self-criticism, the flaws, you have to make a sort of *credo* of yourself as Irish. You have to believe that there is in the sum total of our personal histories and our national history, a goodness about us that will allow us to criticise ourselves.

I'd like to say to Mary Henry: the reason she came across such difficulty about criticism is that many people, on hearing criticism of us, hear the old reminder that we are a flawed, inadequate, inefficient, incompetent and doomed to be incompetent people. You even hear it in the discussions of our current traumas about Greencore etc: the notion that we have disgraced ourselves again. Who said that to us? We say it to us. Over in Britain who the hell even notices us, as someone said earlier. They *will* notice if we tell them loud enough that we have disgraced ourselves again.

Mary Henry:
If I could reply to that. Mercifully I feel no terrible self-disgust at the moment. While we have scandals and rightly criticise them, our scandals here are nothing to Japan, nothing to England. (I think we are exaggerating the situation to say that the whole world is looking at them). Nonetheless, I found it a relief that you criticised any part of our culture. But people may dismiss what you say because you worked in England for twenty years. Actually I don't think we are too bad, and have no sense of disgust about being Irish.

Anthony Clare:
I'm a happy Irishman. I'm merely analysing the wider situation.

Mary Henry:
Yes, I understand you, but I doubt that the majority of Irish people are quite so tortured.

Chairman:
Well, let's see. Who's tortured and who isn't tortured?

Lelia Doolan:
I'm not tortured – I don't think I'm tortured. I don't know how I would describe myself. I'm a kind of a kaleidoscopic farrago: Atlantean or Celtic, depending on whether you are a Bob Quinnite or not. Anyway, I remember a poem of Donagh MacDonagh's called 'Dublin Made Me' and I was thinking, when Mary Robinson was talking, about Pearse and the way in which we are constructed by the past – which I don't completely accept. I think we are certainly constructing ourselves, but I would imagine that the past is merely some of the mortar and bonding and cement and straw,

yet the present is another great part of that. And looking at my
own history, in as much as one has a personal history, I'm a
product of a Dublin and a Clare background: traditional nonconformist Catholic, aspiring, self-improving, ex-rural middle-class.
I suppose it took exposure to a tremendous amount of influences
and happenings and family and friends to make the changes
which to me are a part of every human life. Either we decide to be
closed and fixed and finished or we are endlessly making and
remaking ourselves.

I had a hatred of anything to do with the Bog Irish, as I thought,
when I was a snobby adolescent Loreto girl. I slowly became a
different kind of person through exposure to the theatre, to Irish
speakers, to my own past, to my own family. I became, when
leaving television, aware of the complacent middle-class self-satis-
faction which I had practised as a member of a large organisation.
I also experienced complete confusion in relation to the institution of religion when I looked at the life and the history of people
in the North of Ireland, where I went to live for four or five years
in the Seventies. I became aware of the depth of my ignorance,
which I think I have only made the slightest repair of here and
there, and which needs continual maintenance. This is because
the further away one is from the North, the less frequently one
goes there, the less opportunity you have to allow that part of
the leaven in your system to rise. So, as a constantly shifting,
changing, oscillating, if you like, human person (which I think us
all to be), living in the West of Ireland, I would stress an area
which I hope will get a certain attention. That is the area of
education.

I recently came across the Schools Collection, which you probably heard a lot about recently in the papers, and which was a
tremendous and amazing imaginative stroke on the part of people
in the Folklore Commission in Dublin. They decided to turn the
national schools of Ireland into research stations for the recovery
of the local life within which each school lived. The result was an
astonishing archive, some of which has been on view in UCD
recently, of childrens' essays on every aspect of life: on the care of
the feet, on lucky days, on legends of the locality, on beliefs, on
prayers, on agricultural matters, on naming the parts of tackle of a
horse. That is, on all of those things which to me are 'culture' and
are the culture of people at a certain point of their development.
It is a saddening fact that that kind of learning no longer forms

part of the curriculum of Irish schools. I asked in a number of places around the Burren, whether or not this was something that they would be interested in doing. There was a huge response of interest and a sense of loss that this hadn't really been done or thought of. I'm hoping that that experience of mine and the experiences that you are going to talk about in education will perhaps persuade us forward into localisation – which is not a narrow thing, you know, because the amazing thing about that exhibition is its universality.

I am quite sure that the guilt or non-guilt that we may feel from time to time is a universal, and that Ireland is neither a closed entity nor – and I hope this weekend will show it – merely a male or a middle-class or middle-aged entity. I hope that all those things that you have been talking about , Desmond, such as the disco culture of the country will also be taken into account, including their mobility within the whole island.

Chairman:
Certainly it is our intention that culture should be discussed in that way and on those levels.

Now, Brendan Kennelly has told me that he can recite the poem to which Lelia Doolan referred: Donagh MacDonagh's 'Dublin Made Me'.

Brendan Kennelly:
Yes, and it's a poem that I deliberately memorised. I had a chat with Terence Brown who will be talking tomorrow and I mentioned the poem to him, and he said 'Christ that's an ignorant poem'. It is a middle-class, middle-aged, Catholic, bigotted, judging poem and I like it. Why? Because when I meet a Dublin man or a Belfast man, or a Parisian of a certain kind, and I taste their bigotted pride in their own place, it terrifies me and it attracts me.

DUBLIN MADE ME

Dublin made me and no little town
With the country closing in on its streets
The cattle walking proudly on its pavements
The jobbers, the gombeenmen and the cheats,

Devouring the fair-day between them
A public-house to half a hundred men
And the teacher, the solicitor and the bank-clerk
In the hotel bar drinking for ten.

Dublin made me, not the secret poteen still,
The raw and hungry hills of the West
The bare road flung over profitless bog
Where only a snipe could nest

Where the sea takes its tithe of every boat.
Bawneen and currach have no allegiance of mine,
Nor the cute, self-deceiving talkers of the South
Who look to the East for a sign.

The soft and dreary midlands with their tame canals
Wallow between sea and sea, remote from adventure,
And Northward a far and fortified province
Crouches under the lash of arid censure.

I disclaim all fertile meadows, all tilled land
The evil that grows from it and the good,
But the Dublin of old statutes, this arrogant city,
Stirs proudly and secretly in my blood.

There is also what I would call a beautiful Protestant poem about Dublin, which is a much more civilised poem. It's by Louis MacNeice, who felt outside in Dublin. Now Dublin is a great city for making you feel an outsider. I've been here over thirty years, and every morning when I come out one of the porters says to me: 'Are you going home to snag the turnips?' And, you know, they never let you forget. Anyway, this is MacNeice's poem, and I think of it as Protestant. I mean: enlightened, lonely, sensitive, not belonging, peripheral, mystical, grateful for little crumbs, extremely perceptive.

from **DUBLIN**

This was never my town,
I was not born nor bred
Nor schooled here and she will not
Have me alive or dead
But yet she holds my mind

With her seedy elegance,
With her gentle veils of rain....

The lights jig in the river
With a concertina movement
And the sun comes up in the morning
Like barley-sugar on the water
And the mist on the Wicklow hills
Is close, as close
As the peasantry were to the landlord,
As the Irish to the Anglo-Irish,
As the killer is close one moment
To the man he kills,
Or as the moment itself
Is close to the next moment.

She is not an Irish town
And she is not English,
Historic with guns and vermin
And the cold renown
Of a fragment of Church latin,
Of an oratorical phrase.
But oh the days are soft,
Soft enough to forget
The lesson better learnt,
The bullet on the wet
Streets, the crooked deal,
The steel behind the laugh,
The Four Courts burnt.

Fort of the Dane,
Garrison of the Saxon,
Augustan capital
Of a Gaelic nation,
Appropriating all
The alien brought,
You give me time for thought....

Chairman:
I'm somewhat troubled because the artists, if we include psychiatry
as an art, have spoken of and celebrated openness, but there must
be amongst us people who fear openness, who know they fear

openness, and could perhaps tell us of their experience of fearing openness. Would anyone like to approach our task from that point of view?

Joseph Liechty:
I am on the convening committee for this event. I am very comfortable with saying the problem is closed minds. But I am uncomfortable with saying that the solution is open minds. By Brendan's own standards, progress comes through the union of opposites. Therefore an open mind can't be the solution, it's the opposite problem. An open mind can be very little different from an empty mind, and if you had grown up in the US in the late Sixties and early Seventies as I did, you would feel the force of that equation. At the same time, a closed mind can simply be discernment gone to seed. So how do we get discernment and openness together? That's as difficult an equilibrium as living in social harmony.

Brendan Kennelly:
Does anyone want to answer that? Well, what I was trying to say was that my mind is closed in many many ways, and unconsciously closed, which is terrifying. If, for example, I was to admit that at this stage of my life, in my fifty-fifth year that I am basically incapable of forming a decent relationship with a woman, that's true, and I'm not particularly confessional. I tried marriage, I tried all sorts of relationships. I admire women immensely but I distrust my admiration, because it's not based on an ability to relate properly. I tried to write a play about them. I wrote a play in St Pat's when I was in with alcoholism listening to women reaching heights and depths of sublime obscenity cursing Irish men. It was a play in which I put all the self-loathing that Anthony Clare talks about into the man who was simply myself and the men who refuse to visit their women. That kind of closed mind, that kind of zipped mind, as it were, where you just cannot relate – that's Irish, the real Irish thing. When Anthony Clare was talking about the gift of words, the gift of language, he was dead right. An awful lot of the love of poetry and the ability with it, with literature and with words is in fact a measure of the closed mind, and a measure of emotional evasiveness. And I would say, listening to what he said there, that the more articulate and eloquent you find yourself being, the more something else inside you is saying 'You're closed – you can't really relate, you walked out on her, she walked out on you, you

failed to say so many things, you couldn't really accept her full femininity, you couldn't really make love to the full person'. I often ask Irishmen: 'How many good nights of love have you had in your life?' and after about three pints they will say: 'I think there was one in 1956 where . . .' you know. So much of Irish relationship is a shambles, but a respectable shambles, or a drunken shambles, or an articulate shambles.

And that's – I have no hesitation in saying these things – connected with the quality of our politics, the quality of our teaching. An awful lot of good teaching is born out of your desperation, and a lot of good poetry is born out of the mess that you are. I would say that a lot of politicians, a lot of good academics, are total fakes as human beings. I know a lot of academics, and they are fake buggers the lot of them, because they are just a kind of footnotes to reality – to real living. I see all that in myself.

People ring me: just because you come out and say you're an alcoholic or you say you're a depressive. People ring you from all over the country. I get five or six letters every day from men and women who say the whole range of the thing. So the closed mind has value just as, as I tried to say, betrayal has value. If you didn't betray, you wouldn't know the meaning of trust, which is why forms in the middle – like the middle class of any idea or emotion – are basically the science of playing it safe, and we need people who play it safe.

Mari Fitzduff (Community Relations Council, Northern Ireland): I think at least I score in being a woman. Brendan has said our time has come and I will take some of it now. I have lived twenty years in the Republic and twenty years in the North. I'm not so sure we're afraid of openness. I think we are afraid, North and South, male and female, of being in charge – of being responsible. And I think that is partly what being a small island beside a big island did to us. At some level there were others who were in charge – when it wasn't the English it was the Church. A theme runs through: there is somebody else who is responsible or who will be responsible.

The big change, I suggest, that has happened in the North is that we have realised the 'Superdaddies' don't actually have the answer, whether they are in Dublin or in London. And that ultimately it is going to be up to us – male and female, Protestants and Catholics. I have worked with therapists who had to train across the water. Many of them were Protestants and they were as secure in their inferiority as the Catholics were, so that's something they had in common. But I think we're rapidly learning. When you discover that they don't have the answers, you actually realise (after a tremendous time of fear and transition) that what you come up with is of use. I think it's through people like Brendan Kennelly, through our dramatists, our poets, that we are coming into our own. If any of us go across to the States we find out how we are valued in being Irish. Indeed, even if you go across the water and discover what you can do to a night with people there by being Irish you discover it's not that we are less, it's that we are different, and we shouldn't give up those differences. Maybe we would need to add to it by recognising that there are messes, there are worse scandals, elsewhere and I think we need to address that as well.

Mary Holland (*Irish Times*):
I would like to echo very strongly some of what Brendan had to say. I've had an astonishing experience in the last couple of weeks. It's something that dates actually from the Abortion referendum, and I felt really embarrassed at dragging it up again. During or just prior to the Abortion referendum I said in print that I had had an abortion, and perhaps other women would be prepared to come out and say that they had had an abortion: perhaps we might at least be able to put a human face on the problem in that way. I didn't want to bring it up again, because it is absurd that a woman who is just past childbearing age is still apparently the only woman in Ireland who has had an abortion. Still I felt that I had to do it in the context of what I was writing about, which was the laws about homosexuality. I was writing about how we live always with a situation where things are accepted, even if disgraceful or illegal, as long as you don't rock the boat. As Jennifer was saying, it's OK, you are allowed to get on with your life provided you don't 'come out'. I said in the context of the whole debate about outing: 'Surely there must be lots of people in Ireland who are homosexual, whom it would not damage in any way if they were to make a gesture and not make a tremendous thing about it, but in some way let it be known that they were prepared to be public about their homosexuality. I'm not suggesting that everyone is an Ian McKellen and has to take it up as a cause.

I felt that I had to say: 'Look, it isn't appalling'. Then I got placards with murder and all that sort of thing , but what upsets

me really has been the response from women who come up to me
in the streets who can't know me, except from my face at the top of
a newspaper column, and say: 'Thank you for saying it'. And now
young men too come up to me and say: 'Thank you for writing
about being gay in that way'. It is just absolutely appalling to me,
that these people are getting comfort for something that they
cannot talk about, presumably, in their lives. Traumatic experiences, and they are looking for some kind of comfort from a
newspaper column. I don't know if any of you have read the piece
in the *Irish Times* from a young English doctor in a casualty department where he asked: 'What do doctors do in Ireland?' But of
course, it isn't just what doctors do (or don't do) that forces young
women to go through this on their own. The young woman says to
a young doctor in the casualty department: 'I have to catch the
boat, it would be terrible if my parents knew – my father would
rather I was dead than pregnant.' People lead lives of terrible,
hidden desperation – where they just have to wipe out experiences, rather than try to learn to cope with them. And if Anthony
Clare wonders why people have self-disgust and self-hatred, I suppose those are some of the reasons. I think the rest of us have a
duty to try and make it easier for them to live lives in the open.

Margaret MacCurtain:
I think I should follow that, by saying that I am a celibate. In the
1960s I discovered in Canon Law that I was a sister and a lay
person, a celibate and not a nun. I have much in common with
Jennifer Johnston in her description of what it was to be raised in
Ireland in the 1930s and 1940s, although I was living in Kerry. I
recognised common strands in many of the experiences she was
talking about, such as my brothers going to public school in North
Kerry and sisters staying put at home. I remembered the time
when my father who was the Inspector of Schools (I was about
eight or nine) brought us down in the car to Dunquin on the day
when he closed officially, in the name of the Department of
Education, the primary school on the Great Blasket. I hope we will
be self-indulgent in sharing reminiscences this weekend. Now I
would like to pick up something implicit in Brendan Kennelly's
words: I believe a new Ireland developed in the 1960s for me,
when I turned into a sister from being a nun.

It was a very painful time for me because, at the beginning of the
1960s, we religious women were faced with the whole crashing

down of a monolithic Catholic church. I was in Rome doing a doctorate in those years of good old Pope John XXIII. It was a tremendous experience because for the preparatory sessions for a Vatican council, experimental workshops drew from young sisters and students their feelings about celibate life, about the church in that period. To give you some idea of the innocence of somebody who had entered religious life in the early 1950s after university and after boyfriends, I remember asking an American girl: 'What is the meaning of 'Never on Sundays' – it was a film showing in Rome at the time.

The 1960s are an experience that we should examine closely. I can only speak from my own experience, which was at the beginning of the Sixties when I was an innocent abroad – even though Roma di notte teaches one a lot even when looking from a bus that goes out to holy places of pilgrimage in North Italy! But by the end of the Sixties I was wide awake. A lot of my friends had left the religious life to marry. Some of the priests and brothers I loved had gone off and had married. Some of the sisters who were my closest friends abandoned religious life in the 1970s and I felt myself in the middle Seventies very desolate. These friends would sometimes ask me: 'What are you hanging on for?'.

Shall I tell you what I'm hanging on for? I'm hanging on for the final crash of that monolithic church of the early Sixties before Vatican II. There is a paradigm shift: it is about women discovering that their history, certainly in the Republic, but I expect in the whole island, began sometime in the 1960s and it began with the recovery of our sexuality. I should tell you honestly the celibates also discovered their sexuality if they had any sense at all, which they had, in the Sixties and in the Seventies. They discovered whether they were gay or lesbian, or whether they were heterosexual – or else they kept a closed mind. Many of those who didn't discover their sexuality and kept their closed minds are, I suspect, the bishops of this country who are part of the monolith. I am very grateful to Northern Ireland because you have forced the South to make a paradigm shift, and the North is still forcing the pace. But what I would like to discover is a little light at the end of the tunnel when we go away tomorrow night – what are we paradigm shifting towards?

Desmond Fennell :

Mr Chairman, what I was worried about when I spoke earlier was not the lectures tomorrow morning: knowing the quality of the two men in question, I look forward to their lectures. But what I am worried about is that after the free-for-all of this hour's discussion, where we have such a variety of the Irish experience offered to us by so many people, we should be forced to continue our discussion in the Procrustean beds of Irish-Ireland and British Ireland and to talk in those frameworks. I would therefore put it to you that, as Chairman, you might consider whether that is the best framework for having us continue the discussion that has begun here this evening.

Chairman:
Ten minutes from the end of the discussion, I don't think it would be advisable to change the rules.

Desmond Fennell:
I'm not talking about this discussion. I'm talking about tomorrow. If you look at the programme you'll see that. We will divide up and either talk about Irish-Ireland or we will talk about British Ireland – those are the only two themes offered to us, the only two frameworks for discussion tomorrow morning. I think they leave out so much and that is evidenced by what we are hearing.

Chairman:
Well, I don't think they do. I think they are two very large themes that can include everything that should be discussed and I have total trust in the good sense of the participants in this conference. I take your point, and I have no doubt the audience here would take your point, and took it before, I suspect, it was made. Ten minutes to go, before we break. Now, this is a most important stage of the conference, because this is an occasion when you can drop suggestions into the assembly so that they can be germinating overnight.

Robin Wilson (editor of *Fortnight*):
That what has happened in the North has brought about this debate in the South may be true in the very narrow sense of this particular conference. But it seems to me to be nonsense in the sense of the argument that has gone on on this side of the border about cultural politics, which goes back well before the beginning of the troubles. Most people date it to the late 1950s and early 1960s, with Lemass, the Programme for Economic   Expansion,

etc. The impact of the North on the South has, for the most part, as everyone knows, been to turn off people in the South from the North and its violence. I'm quite disappointed with the general tenor of this debate, to be quite honest, apart from the comments that Mary Holland made, which I would strongly endorse. If, as Paddy said at the outset, we want to see a situation where the violence is brought to an end, I can't say if I was a member of a paramilitary organisation in Ireland, and I heard this discussion, that I would feel terribly threatened by it.

I think that what it rather disturbingly tells us is the tendency to be quite happy among ourselves in Ireland with a level of discussion which is anecdotal, which is very superficial, and which, for example, has so far not been participated in by anybody who is a sociologist, who is a critical theorist, social theorist, whatever. This strikes me as absolutely bizarre, that a debate about culture can take place, and which in any other country would immediately involve all those other kinds of people, and none of them have been involved. For that reason, we have accepted, as Desmond rightly says, quite monolithic notions. One speaker said that our scandal is maybe, as Charlie Haughey said, not much worse than other people's scandals. What do they mean by 'our' scandals? We are not all Michael Smurfits or Dermot Desmonds or those other characters. The fact that there are scandals involving those people is to do with various things, one of which is class, the class divide in Ireland. It is that monolithic kind of thinking which seems to me to be a major problem in another sense – and this is where I would bring in the North.

If you look at the programme for the workshops tomorrow there is a very telling use of the word 'we'. There is a reference in the workshop rubric in the British Ireland workshop that says: 'How can they help us relate to Unionists' – that immediately defines Unionists as non-Irish or lesser Irish people or Irish only on a kind of grace and sufferance. And it then says at a further point: 'Which bits of British Ireland do we like?' – the implication being that we are 'we', are not part of them. All I would say is that far from the idea that there's too much self-criticism, there is far too little self-criticism about the cultural context North and South. And, finally, regarding Mari Fitzduff's point, I would be happy to accept it if I wasn't so aware of all the numbers of ways that Ireland – North and South – has been changed by external influences, some of which have been fought for by our President, and one of which – the legalisation of homosexuality in the North, and its eventual legalisation in the South – is entirely a product of the external influence of the European Court of Human Rights.

Niall Crowley (Honorary Chairman):
On a point of information: Robin Wilson is wrong in his interpretation of that sheet. 'We' means people in the Irish Republic talking about their own cultural complexity in relation to other cultures and other situations. It's a totally valid use of the words 'us' and 'we' and it doesn't make any judgements or in any way insult anybody nor is it intended to do so.

I would also like to say while I'm on my feet that it's easier to have a closed mind than an open mind. It's much more comfortable – much more relaxing. It might be more interesting to have an open mind if you actually made the effort, but it is very hard to sustain that effort.I find that I have a closed mind and I had a closed mind. I have had it prised open occasionally by my children, and it gets excited by the ideas that they inject and I embrace them and perhaps they become part of me, but my mind tends to rapidly snap closed again, into a more comfortable posture. That might apply to a lot of us. I think also that we have a lot to learn from our children. I would hope, therefore, that the new generation of Irish men and women will have much more open minds than their elders had.

John Waters (*Irish Times*):
I would like to take up the crucial question which Margaret MacCurtain asked: What is the nature of the change that is happening? I think it is very important for us to recognise that we are at the point of change – that we are at a crossroads. She mentioned that the 1960s began something, and I think we could make the mistake of thinking that the Sixties began the present. I think the Sixties began a different past to the one before that, and what we have been witnessing for the past twenty or thirty years has been a backlash to the previous past. What we have been fighting is a battle between two pasts, and now we are at the point of the present, going into the future. And I think that all the signposts we see at the crossroads are pointing in a particular direction.

The President spoke earlier about the community groups she addresses all over the country, and she has been making these speeches to them for a year and a half now. There is a level of activity happening all over the country, which we aren't necessarily aware of. It doesn't appear on television, it isn't talked about in the Dáil, but people are actually talking to each other about these very ideas which we are discussing – just as we are talking in this room now. People in Headford and Ballyhaunis and Ballaghadreen and Charlestown: and in all these places people are talking about, and thinking, the same things. I think we should all realise that, even though there hasn't been affirmation for that process, it is actually happening. The other signpost as well, the President, I think is a symbol of that. There is a coming of age, of our nation, our independence. Our present generation of politicians who, if you like, defined the period when we had that battle between the two pasts, are reaching retirement age. However, some of them are anxious to conceal the fact that the coming of age, the change, means anything, and promising that they will go on like Chinese leaders.

But I think we can actually see through that now, and there are all kinds of indicators which, if we begin to look and see them for what they are, will give us a sense of where we need to go. This morning on the radio I heard Dr Conor Cruise O'Brien talking about a book which Paddy MacEntee mentioned earlier, a book about Parnell. He was talking about the two Irelands – Dublin, along the East coast, and the rest of Ireland – and he said you could define it as Parnell Ireland and anti-Parnell Ireland. He said that that division was still in existence, and he linked it with President Robinson. I think he actually put one of his fingers on it but not two. I think you need two. Yes, there are changes, but I doubt whether Parnell is of any relevance. That is a mistake we have been making – we have been taking all our signs from the past. I think it would be much more appropriate if we talked about modern Ireland in terms of Sawdoctors Ireland and anti-Sawdoctors Ireland. Those are much more real definitions of the country that we live in now.

Chairman:
Before we adjourn, I would suggest that what Robin Wilson said is of very great importance. I think we might very well stop here, and one of the things that we might think about overnight is what Robin Wilson said.

AFTER-DINNER SPEECH BY MR CHRIS FLOOD TD, MINISTER OF STATE

Introduction – Niall Crowley, Hon. Chairman

The Cultures of Ireland Group which was initiated by Co-Operation North is especially pleased that An Taoiseach Mr Charles Haughey has endorsed our conference and asked Mr Chris Flood, Minister of State at the Department of Health, to attend representing the Irish Government. I would like, firstly, to welcome Mr Flood.

It is especially important that Mr Flood is here, and members of various Government Departments, as this conference aims to provide approaches which might lead to the implementation by various Government Departments of programmes of mutual understanding and tolerance – particularly in the spheres of education and the environment.

It is especially heartening that the Department of the Environment has recently empowered Local Authorities to spend some of their funding on twinning programmes. As you know, Co-Operation North, our sister organisation, has twinned Newry and Mourne District Council with Clare County Council, and Moyle District Council with Ballinasloe U.D.C. on the basis of a programme of mutual understanding and respect, with the support of all political groupings. We would like to see Government or Local Government Programmes specifically dealing with Councils North and South of the border.

We would also like to see programmes for mutual understanding and respect introduced into our schools curriculum, especially in the areas of social science and history.

Ideally, we would like the Irish Government to form a counterpart to the Community Relations Council in Northern Ireland, a body similar in constitution to the Arts Council, that would advise on and implement cross-border initiatives. I will now hand you over to Mr Flood to say a few words.

MR CHRIS FLOOD TD

Distinguished Guests, Ladies and Gentlemen.

I am happy to join other speakers in welcoming this Conference on the Cultures of Ireland. Much has been said today which has been thought-provoking and I am sure that tomorrow's discussions will be equally stimulating.

I am particularly glad that the Conference is being held during a year in which the contribution which Dublin has made to European culture is being recognised. The European dimension is in many ways relevant to our reflections. Central to the process of European integration since the War has been an acceptance of cultural diversity. That principle is today even more important than before, as we observe developments in the Soviet Union and in Eastern Europe. No political stability can be achieved by the suppression of legitimate political and cultural aspirations.

It is a tribute to the energy of the principal organiser, Constance Short, and to the vision of all those who launched this Conference, that we have here tonight such a diverse gathering of representatives from the worlds of politics, the arts, academic life and the Churches. Most importantly, perhaps, we have a cross-section of people from both sides of the border and from a variety of political and ideological backgrounds.

As Irishmen and Irishwomen, we must all live with the burden of our history. There is a legacy of suspicion and misunderstanding which cannot be set aside easily or quickly. Dialogue is the key to resolving these tensions and to building a new Ireland together. We must begin by talking to, and listening to, each other. We cannot hope to solve our problems unless we engage in a process of dialogue. Gatherings such as this make a valuable contribution to this dialogue. They enhance mutual understanding and trust and strengthen the bridges between our various traditions.

Tolerance and respect for the right to be different are fundamental values in any civilised society. It is only through the accommodation of difference that we can break down barriers between people and remove the prejudice and ignorance which have bedevilled our history. The poet W. H. Auden has observed that 'all real unity commences in consciousness of differences'.

Lately we have seen increased recognition of this principle. Within the past couple of years, two conferences have been held in

Northern Ireland under the auspices of the Central Community Relations Unit, which explored the concepts of 'Irishness' and 'Britishness'. In addition, courses such as 'Education for Mutual Understanding' and 'Cultural Heritage' have been introduced to the school syllabus. It is to be hoped that such initiatives will help to spread a deeper understanding of, and respect for, the various political and cultural traditions which exist on this island.

The challenge to embrace difference, to recognise that the rights and aspirations of others are no less valid and no less compelling than our own, is one which we must all address. I am confident that this Conference will play a valuable role in this process and I wish the organisers and the participants every success.

PART II

IRISH IRELAND/BRITISH IRELAND

CHAIRMAN'S INTRODUCTION

There is a long programme today, and before calling on this morning's distinguished speakers, I think it appropriate to make a very few remarks about yesterday evening's proceedings.

Jennifer Johnston in her contribution yesterday, gave us a very subtle metaphor for the problems of the Protestant growing up in this state. I fear that in our debate yesterday evening the problems identified by Jennifer were not addressed, and perhaps we could try to address them today, or some of them.

Brendan Kennelly's contribution yesterday explored the recognition of 'otherness' as the key to cultural tolerance. It seems to me that before we can recognise 'otherness' we need to have a firm grasp of our own reality. Conor Cruise O'Brien talks about the inhabitants of this part of the island as 'suffering from chronic low level fantasy'. Our function here is to get behind fantasy to the realities, so that having grasped the realities, we can go the step further and recognise the cultural realities of our neighbours in Northern Ireland. I believe it is important to realise that we in this state are regarded with fear and suspicion by those same neighbours.

I suggest that we should examine honestly the origins and the nature of these fears and suspicions. We must also examine the fears and suspicions that we have here of various cultural groups in Northern Ireland. And we must not lose sight of the fact that we are meeting in a context of murder, death and destruction.

We have two distinguished speakers here this morning. Gearóid O'Tuathaigh is an historian and he will examine the historic strands in, and debate about, the cultural particularity of Irishness defined by those describing themselves, or described by others as Irish Irelanders. Professor O'Tuathaigh is a cultural historian – a specialist in emigrant history. He is Associate Professor of History at University College Galway. He is the author of a study of Ireland before the famine, and a co-author with Joe Lee of *The Age of De Valera.*

Our second speaker this morning will be Terence Brown. He is a literary critic and cultural historian and will examine how British culture has affected Irish life since partition, together with the significance of this relationship for current debates about Irish identity. Terence was born in China, educated in Belfast, and is Associate Professor of English at Trinity College Dublin. He is the author of the extremely influential study *Ireland: A Social and Cultural History 1922-85, Northern Voices* and, most recently, *Ireland's Literature.*

PROFESSOR GEARÓID Ó TUATHAIGH

The Irish-Ireland Idea: Rationale and Relevance

With the final disappearance of the Celtic languages there will be no further excuse for referring to the peoples of Brittany, Ireland, Scotland, and Wales as Celts, for there was never any justification other than the linguistic one for the appellation. Without their languages the populations of these countries will more easily lose their identity and be absorbed into the dominant cultures of Britain or France, ultimately to be swallowed up in a greater European identity. Thus will end a cultural and literary tradition which reaches back on the islands of Britain and Ireland to the end of the Roman Empire. This will be the first time that a European linguistic family with such a long and distinguished literary history will have passed into oblivion.[1]

※※※

May I begin with a brief word, defining certain terms of reference? I use 'culture' in a conventional sense, as an 'independent noun, whether used generically or specifically, which indicates a particular way of life, whether of a people, a period or a group'.[2] The cultural particularity to be understood in the term 'Irish culture' is a function of the ethnicity of the group being discussed (rather than, for example, a function of class or gender). I take ethnicity to be a cultural construct, a version of themselves which different peoples adopt, emphasise and proclaim as evidence of their distinctive identity as a people.[3] The selection of elements or cultural characteristics which make up this version of ethnicity cannot, of course, be a matter of casual choice: the cultural traits claimed as distinctive must be meaningful for the people making the claim and must be recognised by others (i.e. externally validated) as constituting distinguishing marks for the purpose of cultural differentiation. In the field of anthropological or sociological enquiry, the phrase 'Irish culture' might be taken to mean the total system – the 'designs for living' – through which life is lived by Irish people in Ireland. For the purposes of this conference, however, I feel it will be more helpful to concentrate on those aspects of Irish ethnicity – the key constituents of Irish 'identity' – which have been a subject of debate and of dispute in Ireland for a considerable time and which continue to perplex not only Irish people, but many other people also, in our own day.

The relationship between culture, identity and tradition in modern Ireland has for some considerable time now been the focus of complex debate. Since the later 1960s an unusually varied company of Irish writers and scholars of different backgrounds–personal, social and intellectual – have been addressing this debate, and the outcome has been a rich interrogation of the Irish cultural predicament – in its historical and contemporary settings. It is not an intention here to offer a digest of the main points at issue in this debate.[4] But, for all the variety of perspectives that characterise contributions to the debate, there has emerged a common view of the Irish tradition 'as divided, discontinuous and founded on a problematic identity'. While it would be invidious to single out any particular contribution as having had a decisive influence in dictating the terms of the debate, nevertheless the text which first sought to situate the debate in a firm historical context was the late F.S.L. Lyons's *Culture and Anarchy in Ireland* (first published in 1979). Lyons had set up an opposition between 'cultural fusion' or 'a unity of being' as an enterprise of intellectuals in the generation after Parnell, and cultural disintegration, 'an anarchy in the mind and in the heart', which (tragically in Lyons's view) was what presaged the great fragmentation and divisions in the period 1912–22. It is worth quoting Lyons's verdict:

> An anarchy that sprang from the collision within a small and intimate island of seemingly irreconcilable cultures, unable to live together or to live apart, caught inextricably in the web of their tragic history.[5]

Roy Foster has described Lyons's book as 'tremendously influential', 'in many respects (his) best book'; and has claimed that Lyons's view of cultural conflict/anarchy became 'in a sense,

entrenched – partly because of the persuasive and authoritative
nature of Lyons's writing, and his own great stature as a historian'.
But Foster himself, for all his admiration for Lyons, finds the
model of cultural conflict/ anarchy as the only alternative to
'fusion' unacceptable, offering a false choice; and he argues instead for an option for 'creative cultural diversity' in Ireland.[6]

In all of the current debate upon cultural identity, what is
remarkable is the way in which the discussion inevitably – and
correctly – harks back to an earlier debate on precisely these same
issues of culture, identity and tradition in the period between c.
1886 and 1922. One outcome of that debate was, in a particular
sense, the establishment of an Irish national State proclaiming an
official 'Irish identity', a distinctive Irish 'design for living'.

The Irish-Ireland idea is generally understood to mean that set
of propositions and proposals on 'Irish national identity' which
emerged in the period c. 1880–1914 from a number of groups and
organisations in Ireland, all of them sharing a belief that the signs
and substance of Ireland's cultural particularity or distinctiveness
were rapidly disappearing before a tide of 'Anglicisation', with the
result that Irish cultural life was becoming rapidly a vulgar, derivative and provincial outcrop of English culture. The evidence of
accelerating decline of the Irish language as a living vernacular in
Ireland was, perhaps, the most concrete proof of the cultural
change being lamented and denounced. But the dominance of
what were seen as English norms and standards in the artistic,
intellectual, leisure and even commercial life of Ireland also loomed
large on the charge sheet: a cultural dominance and homogenisation which was reaching into popular as well as élite culture, as a
consequence of the changes in literacy, communication and travel
(including migration and emigration) which had contributed in
the later nineteenth century to the creation of what was, in effect,
a single integrated, cultural zone covering Britain and Ireland. In
short, if cultural change occurs, as the anthropologists tell us,
through a combination of innovation, improvisation and imitation, the charge of 'Irish-Ireland' was that imitation alone was at
play in the cultural transformation of Victorian Ireland.

These views were shared, in different degrees and with varying
emphasis, by an assortment of groups in the later decades of the
nineteenth century: not only the Gaelic League, the Gaelic Athletic
Association, the writers and intellectuals of the Irish Literary Revival, the ideologues of a cluster of 'advanced nationalist' political

groups (open and clandestine), but also by some advocates of the co-operative movement and by a number of moral re-armament groups organised under Catholic auspices. A strong impulse for cultural nativism combined with a critique of free trade economics to produce an 'import substitution' mentality which attracted a broad spectrum of support. The cultivation of a 'distinctive Irish mind', through the careful nurturing of all the elements of Irish cultural particularity, was the challenging agenda of the Irish-Irelanders. The problem and the debate arose on the criteria for identifying what exactly constituted Irish cultural particularity – what was 'Irishness'. But for all the fury of that debate, up to our own day, we can identify two recurring themes in the various formulations of the Irish-Ireland project: these are the themes of *continuity* and *restoration*. Cultural continuity was the key element in Hyde's case for the Irish language revival.[7] Historically, the theme of 'restoration' was a deeply-rooted motif in Irish nationalist rhetoric (whether the emphasis was on the linguistic or the religious communal sense, or on both): the restoration of Irish society to a pre-conquest, pre-lapsarian state of harmony, wholeness and authenticity (elemental, direct and simple values in contrast to the corrupting compromises fostered by the experience of colonisation).

Given the history of the upheavals of the sixteenth and seventeenth centuries; the evidence of the seemingly inexorable decline of the Irish language (and of the habits, customs and general mentalité associated with the Irish-speaking communities and deemed to be encoded in the language); and, in particular, given the dominant status of English ethnicity within the multi-ethnic British state since the sixteenth century, it was only to be expected that the delineation of a 'distinct and independent Irish mind' in the programme of the Irish-Irelanders would involve a heavy emphasis on differences and contrasts between Irish and English cultural traits, along a broad cultural spectrum. Hyde's call for 'de-Anglicisation' sums up the thrust of the enterprise. Predictably, this obsessive concern with cultural differentiation (or demarcation) from English produced its excesses: a strain of Anglophobia, and a corresponding exaggeration when making claims for the 'superiority' of various Irish cultural forms. There were other interesting, but incidental, by-products of this pre-occupation with cultural demarcation (e.g. rural-urban, innocent-corrupt, spiritual-materialist; all contrasts formulated to subvert negative stereotypes well-entrenched in English cultural commentaries on Ireland). More seriously, the dogmatic native/alien categorisation misunderstood the dynamics of cultural change in a society situated as Ireland was (and is); a highly 'open' society which has the opportunity and the obligation to engage in cultural exchange rather than to retreat into cultural protectionism. The 'Albanian option', so to speak, was never on.

One particular and enduring aspect of the Irish-Ireland project, which has been widely misunderstood, was the desire to relate Ireland's cultural predicament to the experience of other European peoples outside the British sphere, indeed outside the English-speaking world. Apart from stressing the historic, especially the pre-conquest, links between Ireland and the European mainland, the purpose of the European focus of Irish-Ireland propaganda seems to have been the determination to provide a setting for a discussion of cultural relativism more affirmative of Irish self-esteem than the British setting, in which, as a function of political and economic power-structures, Irish ethnicity possessed an inferior status compared to English ethnicity.

I have stressed the variety of groups who contributed to the general Irish-Ireland programme at the turn of the century. The most contentious formulation of the Irish-Ireland idea (and the formulation which actually gave us the title 'Irish-Ireland') was, of course, D.P. Moran's manifesto of 1905.[8] It was Moran who produced the exclusivist definition of Irish cultural identity. For Moran, the Irish nation was, *de facto*, a Catholic nation; its cultural base or matrix was Gaelic, and this matrix must be fortified and developed so as to be capable of absorbing all other 'extraneous' elements which through the centuries had come into the land. This doctrinaire formulation of 'Irishness', the claim for exclusive authenticity for Gaelic-Catholic Ireland, is what is generally understood as the programme of Irish-Ireland, adopted by a cadre of hardline Gaelic Leaguers and Sinn Féiners who became influential in launching and in shaping the ideology of the new Irish state in 1922. Furthermore, it is widely accepted that this exclusivist Irish-Ireland ideology was dominant, not only in the official rhetoric but more pervasively in the symbols and statutes of the Irish state from the 1920s to, perhaps, the 1960s, with consequences which were divisive and culturally disorientating in independent Ireland and which served to intensify communal division and strife in Northern Ireland.

This critique of the consequences of Moran's formulation of the Irish-Ireland idea calls for closer examination. In particular, we would do well to consider carefully what precisely was the relationship between the 'Gaelic' and the 'Catholic' elements – between language and religion – in the construction of a distinctively Irish 'design for living' (a model cultural 'identikit') both before and after the foundation of the Irish Free State in 1922. It is customary to begin with Hyde. It is also appropriate. Hyde's place in the tradition of 'Protestant Gaelicism' (from late eighteenth-century antiquarianism to the more culturally prescriptive Ferguson, Standish O'Grady, Yeats and his circle) has been discussed by most recent scholars of the Gaelic revival and in the cultural debate on the 'Protestant ascendancy' in modern Ireland. Oliver MacDonagh's summary of Hyde's position within this tradition is especially perceptive:

> He followed Ferguson and O'Grady in presenting the native language and culture as supra-factional and supra-sectarian, a field where Irish Protestant and Catholic could meet as equals in Hibernicism . . . On the other hand he adopted and boldly extended Davis's concepts of cultural separation and hostility . . . Hyde differed from Davis in three respects. First, his de-Anglicisation campaign was proclaimed to be apolitical. Secondly, it was to take the offensive, to aim at the restoration of the vernacular language and the traditional life patterns over the entire country . . . Thirdly, it was a programme of action rather than a *Nation* like system of general exhortation.[9]

There are other important distinctions between Hyde and the tradition of 'Protestant Gaelicism', apart, that is, from his practical programme of language revival. For one thing, we need to remind ourselves of Hyde's view of the relationship between language and thought – between, so to speak, the language question and the formation of 'a distinctive Irish mind'. Hyde (in common with others of his time) saw language not merely as *expressing* thought but as *creating* it. This, in effect, meant that Hyde saw the Irish 'design for living' – or at least the values which would inform that design – as coming ready-made with the language. The restoration of Irish – i.e. the creating of an Irish society in which the Irish language would be the vital instrument of cultural reconstruction – would in itself provide the means for the restoration to a dominant position of a set of simple, direct, authentic values and

feelings, arising organically from the Gaelic past, in place of the
derivative, vulgar, meretricious modes of feeling produced by an
'imposed' English materialist culture. The enormous problems
which are inherent in this formulation of cultural reconstruction
need not detain us here.

But Hyde's was not the only 'design for living' or cultural
construct based on the Gaelic past on offer at the turn of the
century. Eoin Mac Neill, Hyde's co-worker in the foundation of
the Gaelic League, has been identified – quite perceptively – by
John Hutchinson as having had a significantly different basis for,
or at least a different orientation to, his advocacy of a Gaelic revival
as a worthy cultural project for the Irish people in the late nineteenth and early twentieth century.[10] It was the Gaelic civilisation
as suffused by Christian values that attracted Eoin MacNeill. It was
this Christian Celtic vision that he sought to champion as a worthy
exemplar, a high Celtic Christian civilisation capable of providing
the values, the ideas ('an adequate inspiration' as Pearse might
have put it) upon which might be constructed an Irish cultural
regeneration, true to its past and determined to turn from vulgar,
imitative provincialism into the clear light of self-confident, self-
aware, historically-rooted nationhood.

This particular 'design for living' – stressing the island of saints
and scholars, of learning and piety, rather than elemental pagan
valour (Cuchulain) or the unspoilt peasants with their folk-magic,
superstitions and legends – was a design far more likely to appeal
to the Catholic bishops and priests, and to the socially assertive if
culturally insecure Catholic middle-classes, the powerful elements
which provided the leadership of Nationalist Ireland in the Home
Rule era. The Catholic Church leaders had, of course, their own
very definite 'design for living' for 'the Irish people' in the later
nineteenth century – a design that was comprehensively confessional in character, with a strong imperial missionary dimension
to it. With its immense social influence, permeating all aspects of
social life; its hugely impressive base of institutional and human
resources (including a proliferation of new, explicitly Catholic
moral re-armament groups at the turn of the century); *it was
inevitable* that the Catholic Church leadership (clerical and lay)
would have a major say in the 'designs for living' which were likely
to be adopted and to influence the symbols and the statutes of the
Irish national state in prospect (this was precisely what fuelled
Ulster Unionist fears).

What is of interest, however, is the ways in which these various visions – Gaelic and Catholic – at different times and at different points complementary and competing – encountered each other in the generation before 1922, and the accommodations between them which can be identified in the cultural identity encoded as 'Irish national identity' in the Irish Free State. It may be suggested that what happened was that the Catholic confessional design – and its major sponsors – succeeded in co-opting the Gaelic vision to its own grand design for an 'Irish identity' based on a shared historical experience; that this co-option was at all times *conditional* on the Gaelic remaining ancillary to the 'larger' religious enterprise; that the strength of the Gaelic 'deposit' (on the 'national identity' after 1922) was more substantial, in some respects, than many of the early revivalists might have expected, and, in other respects, more limited than many of its later critics/detractors were disposed to claim. There remained, at all times, considerable tensions regarding the precise mix of elements which were to form the 'design for living' of Nationalist Ireland. We can get an idea of the changing shape of that design by comparing the character and cultural vision of the Home Rule leadership in 1912 (poised for power), with Sinn Féin in 1919 (now the voice of the Irish Nationalist consensus) and with the officially 'established' cultural/national identity of the new Irish state in the 1920s and 1930s.

In discussions of the cultural significance of the displacement of the Irish Parliamentary Party by Sinn Féin as the voice of Nationalist Ireland in the years 1917–20, it is customary to draw attention to the fact that the old parliamentary party held its ground rather better in parts of Ulster than elsewhere in the country. This is generally accompanied by a reference to its more clericalist/ confessional character in Ulster – a more pervasively Catholic 'communal' party – in contrast with Sinn Féin Ireland, where the militant republican element, at least, had a more robustly secular tradition; or, at the very least, had achieved some degree of historical immunisation against episcopal and even priestly strictures. This distinction has some merit; but it mustn't be pushed too far. After all, the Sinn Féin 'popular front' leadership in 1918 saw the wisdom – indeed the desirability – of De Valera going out to meet the bishops in session in Maynooth to secure their support for the anti-conscription campaign; and Sinn Féin accepted Cardinal Logue, the Catholic Primate, as the honest broker between the two Nationalist parties in the share-out of seats in Nationalist Ulster in 1918. This 'supreme insensitivity towards Protestant fears', as Joseph Lee has called it, may, of course, be seen as evidence of the growing pragmatism of Sinn Féin as it became the voice of catch-all, multi-class, 'communal' Nationalist Ireland during 1917–1918. But what this means, in terms of cultural vision or 'designs for living', was that the minority faith of the Gaelic League purists within the reconstructed Sinn Féin would have to come to terms with – to find some accommodation with – a far wider and culturally more 'casual' Nationalist sentiment in the country.

This is not to claim that the post 1917 Sinn Féin was identical in character to the pre-war Redmonite party and movement. It most certainly was not. There had been decisive changes in the character of its leadership, in its declared political/constitutional objectives, in the dominant rhetoric of its economic and, to a degree, social policy; and, of course, its Gaelic commitment was more substantial in content and more assertive in tone. But, for all that, it did seek to 'represent' – in the liberal-democratic sense of that term – Nationalist Ireland; and, as such, it inevitably felt the strong gravitational pull of the dominant elements within that community (the 'winners', as Lee has put it, of the late nineteenth century – the comfortable farmers professional middle-class, priests and shopkeepers).[11] This is of particular significance when we seek to evaluate what elements of the Gaelic 'designs for living', canvassed so passionately in the debate on national identity between the 1880s and 1922, were actually incorporated in the institutions, modes of operation, general ideas and policies of the new Nationalist state presided over by the heirs to the Sinn Féin revolution – Cumann na nGaedheal and Fianna Fáil – from the 1920s to the 1950s.

In a number of areas the State simply adopted the strategies for Gaelicisation already formulated by the Gaelic League in the first decade of the century: thus, for example, the 1922 Constitution (of the Free State) declared that 'the National language of the Irish Free State . . . is the Irish language', while De Valera's constitution of 1937 strengthened this to declare (article 8) that 'the Irish language as the national language is the first official language' of the State; a significant portion of the political leaders of the State in the 1920s and 1930s subscribed to the view that 'the Irish language was the most irrefutable authenticating mark of the historic Irish nation on whose behalf a national state had been demanded', and that its restoration as the main vernacular of the people ought to be the objective of an independent Irish national state'; making the Irish language a compulsory subject within the curriculum in all state-recognised and funded schools at first and second level; that it be required for recruitment to posts in the civil service and for other posts in the State apparatus – all of these policies were consistent with this general view of the obligation to provide a distinctive and authentic Gaelic design for living, and indeed were simply adopting the strategies proposed before independence by the more aggressive elements within the Gaelic League. Likewise, the widespread use of the Irish language (and, indeed, of other Gaelic designs – coinage, icons etc.) in the official symbolisation of the State (names, titles, official seals etc.) was in conformity with the commitment to the Gaelic 'design for living'.

All of this may be seen as a considerable achievement – at least formally – for the Gaelic League idea. Yet, many ardent revivalists at the time and since were not satisfied with the achievements, and it is not too difficult to see why. After 1922, as before, the decisive ethos within Nationalist Ireland was Catholic rather than Gaelic; the ethos pervading its social legislation, its educational system, its delineation of individual and collective rights; its social mores, its public culture. The dominant 'communal' values of Nationalist Ireland were Catholic rather than Gaelic for the simple reason that the most powerful and widely shared 'sense of peoplehood' in early twentieth-century Ireland was religious/confessional rather than linguistic. To the extent that the Irish Nationalist leadership was genuinely representative of Irish Nationalist opinion – as the Irish Parliamentary Party was to 1914, and as Sinn Féin was from 1918 to the Treaty – it meant that the original Gaelic League idea *pur sang* ('the de-Anglicisation of Ireland') would be a minority faith, but would shade into a range of, so to speak, lighter shades of green attitudes towards the language preservation policy in particular and towards the Gaelic design in general. This range would cover a sentimental affection and good will (at low cost or no cost) for the Gaelic ideal; a more serious acceptance of the need for a supportive (State-led) system to ensure, perhaps to encourage, an 'option for Irish' as a 'design for living', a widespread acceptance of Irish as an indelible part of the Irish historical experience and an acceptance of the appropriateness of its employment in the symbolisation – the public dress – of an Irish national state.

Evaluations of the extent and the detailed policies of the Gaelicisation programme of the new State in the 1920s and 1930s, while all pointing up the failure of the larger project of language-revival in the community at large, tend to range in tone from regret to ridicule and rage. Thus, for example, two firm – but otherwise very different – enthusiasts for the original Gaelic League idea – reach the conclusion that: '. . . the greatest indictment one may make against the League: (is) that it did not succeed in effectively moulding the State which it more than any other body had helped to bring into being';[12] or again: 'for the great failure was that, while the Gaelic League did produce a revolution . . . neither it nor the political movement stemming from it evolved an application of its basic insight to the problems of an Irish commu-nity. The central inspiration gradually lost its nourishing power in an adequate Irish State. The aim of re-activating the continuity of tradition which is the life principle of a historic community tended to become merely that of substituting one language for another' . . . leading to a 'withering of the spiritual content of the revival'.[13]

Joseph Lee's view is more complex, but it is clear that he inclines to the view that the loss of the Irish language may have 'affected the national personality by fostering further the inferior-ity complex that required as a reflex compensating–mechanism an exaggerated Anglophobia'. For Lee, the failure of the language revival project of the new Irish State was symptomatic of a more general failure to create, independent 'social thought' – a failure to successfully break free of the incarcerating mould of a colonial dependency culture – provincial, derivative, the passive rather than the drastic element in the shaping of its direction and des-tiny.[14]

On the other hand, against these voices who are essentially sympathetic to the value of Gaelic in creating a healthy sense of Irish identity, we may notice Oliver MacDonagh's uncharacteristi-cally passionate – not to say intemperate – denunciation of the Gaelic policy of the new state as an arid, intolerant, historically improbable effort at cultural imposition. MacDonagh sees it as riddled with bureaucratic contradictions and cruelties, with spe-cial-interest groups and careerism, and generally at odds with the psychic and social reality of large numbers of Irish people – Nationalist as well as Unionist.

These various evaluations naturally reflect personal convictions on the basic ideological assumptions underlying the debate on the relationship between identity, language and history in Ireland. These were precisely the questions which engaged the intellects and energies of many talented men and women in Ireland at the turn of the century. Hyde had declared the Gaelic League to be 'the only body in Ireland which appears to realise the fact that Ireland has a past, has a history, has a literature . . . the only body in Ireland which seeks to render the present a rational continuation of the past'. Leaving aside the difficult question of what exactly 'a rational continuation of the past' may mean, it seems to me that there was nothing unworthy in seeking to restore to the Irish people a fuller, richer consciousness and understanding of their history than was available to the mass of Irish people – educated Irish people – in the late nineteenth century. What is vital, however, was that it should be realised that the past to which Hyde's present – and *ours* – was heir was a complex, tangled past, comprising many different cultural strands.

Declan Kiberd has suggested that history has left the Irish of the present time with access to 'two cultures for the price of one' (with a strong sense of *irony* as its major mark of identity). This throwaway remark is suggestive of more sober formulations of the analytical concepts most useful in discussing culture, identity and a sense of peoplehood (or 'nationality') in modern Ireland. It is not, perhaps, in the problematic (but as yet uninterrogated) concept of 'discontinuity' that we may find our most satisfying explanations of the complexities of Irish cultural identity, but rather in the concept of a plurality of continuities, interlocking, full of complexity, and demanding of those who would investigate or seek to understand them the most generous of cultural sympathies, together with an appropriate armoury of conceptual and linguistic skills.

May I turn, then, in this concluding section of my paper to ask a question which must exercise us today, in an Ireland where contested definitions and competing assertions of identity are contributing to a conflict in Northern Ireland in which murder and menace are an everyday fact of life. Is the notion of 'Irish-Ireland' at all relevant in the Ireland of the 1990s, and if it is, how may we delineate its relevance? My contention would be that the concept of Irish-Ireland retains a relevance for us and that it is likely to continue to do so for the foreseeable future. My contention rests on a number of assumptions, which I will state briefly.

Firstly, while it may seem, in the unfolding development of Europe in the 1990s, that the nation-state is a diminishing force in determining the major political and economic decisions which closely affect the lives of the peoples of Europe, there is no evidence that ethnicity itself (that is, the desire or the need for cultural differentiation on ethnic, notably linguistic, grounds) is a diminishing force in human affairs, in Europe any more than elsewhere in the world. It is possible to imagine a situation where cultural identities may become more rather than less important in Europe than they are even at the present time. The challenges posed to cultural diversity by the logic of the global village and the information society (the concentrations of power and techno-logical capacity, the control of the media and the message) have been debated now for more than a generation. Raymond Williams's memorable phrase, that the challenge to smaller, minority cultures in the new information age was to learn how to become the arrow rather than the target, has found an echo in many parts of the world. In Europe itself, there are those who believe that the logic of the creation of a single market will be a movement towards an increasing degree of cultural homogenisation (in edu-cational curricula no less than in the consumer market of pop culture). Yet, within the main agencies of European 'integration' there is already a public commitment to a policy of cultural diversity. 'Unity in diversity' is the ringing phrase used to an-nounce this cultural vision of the new Europe. It is reasonable to assume that teasing out what exactly this phrase means will soon generate a major debate in a European context (in terms, for example, of the transfer of educational expertise in a single labour market; television 'regulation'; reconciling differences in social norms and legal rights at a local or national level with the increasing role of European agencies to elaborate, most vitally in the courts, a set of 'European' rights and entitlements). Calls for a 'Europe of the Regions', or for measures/structures to bridge the 'democratic deficit' in decision-making, are but exam-ples of the directions which this debate may take in the coming decade. A concern for cultural particularity (most commonly called national identity) will be shown by the larger cultural com-munities – Germans, French, Spanish. But it will be especially important to the smaller (and, historically, more vulnerable) cul-tural communities – the Catalans, the Flemings, the Welsh, and, indeed, the Irish. In short, the European agenda, quite apart from domestic considerations, is likely to ensure that the thinking and talking classes in Ireland will still be obliged to think and talk about 'Irishness' and Irish cultural identity in the decade ahead.

What is clear, however, is that the D.P. Moran exclusivist version of Irish-Ireland is not a credible option for any discussion of Irish identity in the 1990s. Claims to exclusive authenticity for any one strand of the complex cultural heritage of Ireland were a-historical when first made almost a century ago, and their repetition in the intervening years has not helped in fostering understanding or tolerance of cultural diversity on this island, North or South.

Yet, rejection of the exclusivism of Moran, and acknowledgement of the rich complexity and the many paradoxes of Ireland's cultural heritage, does not, it seems to me, require the rejection of the total corpus of ideas and insights which the Irish-Ireland idea generated. In particular, it seems to me that a strong claim can be made for the Irish language as constituting a special and privileged register of Irishness. This privilege derives not from any claim to exclusive authenticity or legitimacy, but to the richness and antiquity of the cultural continuity to which it testifies. It provides unique access to a store of cultural reference throughout the long centuries of recorded history on this island. It puzzles me that many educated people in Ireland, who in other matters acknowledge a respect for the relics and record of the past (monuments, historic buildings, manuscripts) as a sign of a civilised person, have frequently a blind spot when it comes to the Irish language, arguably the most precious living link we have with the past of human society on this island. The Irish language rarely features as part – still less a central part – of the conservationist agenda; attitudes towards its predicament and future prospects I have found to be disappointingly indifferent or hostile among sections of the educated classes otherwise sensitive and enlightened in their attitudes to conservation and heritage issues. It may, of course, be argued – indeed it frequently is argued – that the very exclusivist claims made for Irish by some revivalists together with the shortcomings of some of the formulaic and bureaucratic means employed in the state language policy in the Irish state from the 1920s, produced a strong and predictable reaction, and that this accounts for the switch-off among sections of the educated and not-so-educated classes from any concern for the language. This may be part of the reason for the reluctance to place the Irish language at the centre of the heritage/conservation agenda; but it cannot be the full explanation. For this we must, it seems to me, face up to and begin to interrogate a complex set of fears, prejudices and anxieties which are the problematic part of the legacy of language change in Ireland during the past few centuries.

Old claims to exclusivity are unacceptable. The theme of 'restoration' – in any literal or simple sense of turning back the clock or expunging the cultural deposit of a turbulent history – is a theme more likely to induce nostalgia and paralysis than hope and creativity. But in the spirit of humanistic creativity the Irish language continues to offer Irish people an unique option for self-knowledge and a knowledge of Ireland and its past, as well as a vernacular literature of great richness and beauty. And it is neither anti-modern nor Anglophobic nor perverse to advocate that the cultivation of the Irish language should be undertaken and supported with purpose and pleasure by all those who value cultural diversity and cultural continuity on this island. This humanistic option ought to be available to everybody living in Ireland, irrespective of religious or political affiliation, North or South. It cannot be the exclusive preserve of any one religious community or political grouping. The Irish language advocates must see and proclaim the Irish-Ireland option of the 1990s as an invitation to cultural enrichment rather than as a members-only card with a set of rules on the back. (The extraordinary flowering of Irish traditional music and its easy and confident intercourse with other forms of music is an illustration of how an unmistakably traditional cultural form can develop and evolve in an environment that is, so to speak, culturally pluralistic.) There must be no grounds for the charge of exclusivism; and in this context I am on record as advocating that the G.A.A. should signal its intention of removing the ban on R.U.C. members being admitted to the Association.

But toleration cuts both ways. Those who are suspicious of or hostile to the Irish-Ireland idea, who continue to warn against monochrome definitions of cultural identity, must themselves guard against intolerant dismissal of that which they do not know but yet fear. There is a form of intolerance also in seeking to deny that there is any point or purpose (indeed, in hinting that it may be dangerous and socially divisive) in calling on Irish people to cherish and cultivate those particular marks of Irishness which have a long historical continuity in Ireland and which other peoples acknowledge as being distinctively Irish.

The continuing importance of ethnicity as a burning issue in Irish society, North and South, in the decade ahead, should not, of course, be taken as signifying that ethnicity will be, or has been, the sole, or in many contexts the main, determinant of one's social being: social class and gender are, and will remain, powerful categories for understanding and describing the patterns and structures of social differentiation in Ireland, as elsewhere in the world. But, to the extent that perceptions of ethnic difference fuel communal strife and violence on this island, it is incumbent upon us to find ways in which the richness and diversity of the cultural strands which make up the Irish identity are acknowledged, and their assorted configurations, North and South, accepted as valid and authentic manifestations of contemporary, living Irish culture. This obligation rests, in the first instance, on the thinking classes, who are to be found in every stratum of society. We must not yield to despair. A great deal is already being done by a host of organisations, groups and schemes, to break down long-hardened moulds of suspicion, ignorance and fear between the communities in Northern Ireland and between communities in the North and in the Republic: educational schemes, curricular innovation, holiday exchange schemes, inter-church activities of various kinds. And it would not be difficult to suggest further initiatives which might be helpful: more regular contacts between the Irish and the Scots and Welsh, and an exploration of the full complexity of cultural contrasts and similarities between all the ethnic groups in the islands of Ireland and Britain; a more systematic investigation of the nature and history of specifically English nationalism (it would be helpful if English scholars and intellectuals were to address this issue more explicitly); an openness to the examples of and parallels between the cultural experience and predicament of other peoples and regions in Europe and our own predicament in Ireland. More imaginative curricula in literature, and a special focus on the diasporic experience of the Irish, might raise useful questions in schools, North and South. These, and other initiatives, in which community and church leaders and local cultural 'heroes' can play a decisive role, may help to move our thinking away from its historically-rooted binary terms of contrast and confrontation – British/English *versus* Irish, with all its problematic, but increasingly obsolete, stereotypes (superior/inferior, powerful/powerless, oppressor/oppressed). On a more formal level, it is surely time for us to begin a total overhaul of the 1937 Constitution, twenty-five years after a major all-party review recommended substantial changes in the document; in the light of the seismic changes which have occurred in the intervening years, further delay in undertaking a major overhaul becomes increasingly difficult to justify.

How these changing perspectives – and the strengthening currents of education, in its widest sense – will affect the minds and machinations of those deep in the bunkers of their own intolerant certainties, on both islands, is difficult to predict. Nobody will underestimate the task. But there is no other way for a project of enlightenment to proceed than through open and honest enquiry, imbued with a tolerance of differences of views and opinions. These, in the last analysis, are the only real weapons in the liberal-democratic locker as its seeks to exorcise the demons of prejudice, suspicion and fear.

Notes

1. Gearóid Mac Eoin, 'The Modern Celts', in *The Celts*, edited by Sabatino Moscati, Otto Hermann Frey, Venceslas Kruta, Barry Raftery and Miklós Szabó (Bompiani, Milano, 1991), p. 674.
2. Raymond Williams, *Keywords* (London 1976), p. 80.
3. F. Barth (ed.), *Ethnic Groups and Boundaries* (London 1969). For a useful application of Barth to the Irish debate, see Hilary Tovey, Damian Hannan and Hal Abrahamson, *Why Irish? Irish Identity and the Irish Language* (Dublin 1989).
4. The debate may be sampled in the issues of *The Crane Bag*, the *Irish Review*, the *Field Day* pamphlets, as well as in such texts as Richard Kearney (ed), *The Irish Mind* (Dublin 1985), and Desmond Fennell, *Beyond Nationalism: The struggle against provinciality in the modern world* (Dublin 1985); Richard Kearney (ed.), *Across the Frontiers: Ireland in the 1990s* (Dublin 1988); Gerald Dawe and Edna Longley (eds), *Across a Roaring Hill: The Protestant imagination in modern Ireland* (Belfast 1985).
5. F.S.L. Lyons, *Culture and Anarchy in Ireland 1890–1939* (Oxford 1979), p. 177.
6. Roy F. Foster, 'Varieties of Irishness', in Maurna Crozier (ed), *Cultural Traditions in Northern Ireland* (Belfast 1989), pp 5–24.
7. For Hyde, see Breandán Ó Conaire (ed), *Douglas Hyde: Language, Lore and Lyrics* (Dublin 1986), and the recent biography, Janet E. and Gareth W. Dunleavy, *Douglas Hyde: A Maker of Modern Ireland* (University of California Press 1991).
8. D.P. Moran, *The Philosophy of Irish-Ireland* (Dublin 1905).
9. Oliver MacDonagh, *States of Mind: A Study of Anglo-Irish Conflict 1780–1980* (London 1983), p. 112.
10. John Hutchinson, *The Dynamics of Cultural Nationalism* (London, 1987).
11. For contrasting perspectives, see Tom Garvin, *Nationalist Revolutionaries in Ireland 1858–1928* (Oxford 1987); Brian P. Murphy, *Patrick Pearse and the Lost Republican Ideal* (Dublin, 1991); J.J. Lee, *Ireland 1912–1985: Politics and Society* (Cambridge 1989).
12. B.S. Mac Aodha, 'Was this a social revolution?', in Seán Ó Tuama (ed), *The Gaelic League Idea* (Cork 1972).

13. Brendan Devlin, 'The Gaelic League – A Spent Force?' in Seán Ó Tuama (ed), *The Gaelic League Idea* (Cork 1972).
14. J.J. Lee, 'Society and Culture', in Frank Litton (ed), *Unequal Achievement: The Irish Experience 1957–1982* (Dublin 1982), and more expansively in the work cited n. 11.
15 MacDonagh, *op.cit.* pp. 104–125.

PROFESSOR TERENCE BROWN

British Ireland

The terminology of the topics we have been invited to engage with this morning bespeaks the problematic nature of the subject in hand: cultural traditions. Both Irish Ireland and British Ireland as terms suggest degrees of insecurity and assertiveness that evidence how deeply implicated with anomaly, paradox and instability they both are. For Britain is Britain and Ireland Ireland: two historically distinct geographical entities whose political union in its full form lasted just over one hundred and twenty years. The term Irish Ireland emerged, nevertheless, despite these undeniable facts, as a counter in political discussion and as a rallying cry in nationalist agitation at the end of the nineteenth century to help define a community's awareness of itself as Irish in an indigenous, autochthonous sense. And it adopted this apparent tautology in lively opposition to what was perceived to be the Anglicisation of Irish life. It was a product of a socio/cultural dialectic that saw a nascent Irish cultural nationalism pitted against, not the idea of Britain exercising power through the agency of the Crown and British Government, but against England, the English language and Anglicisation as a subtle (and often not so subtle) pressure to abandon an historic Gaelic identity.

Significantly, the idea of Britain or Britishness played very little part in this process. The foe, as in countless ballads and revolutionary speeches, was England, the source of all Ireland's woes. And to this day the structure of Irish nationalist self-understanding is to see Ireland and Irishness in a bi-polar relationship with England and Englishness, to the neglect of any acknowledgement of the neighbouring island's essentially federalist polity. The concept of Britain or Britishness has very little currency in nationalist Ireland. We exist, do we not in these islands, as far as British/Irish matters are concerned, in a political arrangement curiously designated the 'Anglo-Irish Agreement', as if this political and legislative instrument were not a treaty signed by the prime minister of the British government, which exercises political authority over Wales, Scotland and Northern Ireland as well as England, and the prime minister of the Irish government, which exercises political authority over only part of the island of Ireland. Similarly at a more popular level, in a work of art that seemed to express the folklore and mythology of Irish nationalism at its most instinctive and visceral level, Brendan Kennelly's *Cromwell*(1983), our contemporary *imbroglio* is symbolised as a permanent destructive conversation between the English Lord Protector and an Irish Buffún who cannot escape from the inauthentic definitions of himself thrust upon him by the English tyrant. So despite the pleasing symmetry of this morning's schedule, the terms Irish Ireland and British Ireland are not symmetrical, do not participate in a symbiotic reciprocity that flows both ways.

Irish Ireland is not essentially defined by British Ireland, even if it shares as a term the paradoxical almost oxymoronic linguistic condition of the idea of British Ireland. It is, or more accurately was, a self-conscious attempt to re-Gaelicise an Ireland which had to all intents and purposes been incorporated into the Anglo-Saxon world: an Ireland in which the consciousness of Britain and Britishness had to be suppressed or simply ignored since it might, with its larger, more inclusive definitions of insular identity on the offshore archipelago of Britain and Ireland, have vitiated the polemical thrust of its ideology. Nonetheless, the idea of British Ireland, to a considerable degree, is a product of a reaction against the idea of Irish Ireland and to that extent the social realities to which the terms refer are involved with one another. But the fact that the idea of Irish Ireland as socio/cultural formation takes little account of the British dimension of its defining context, concentrating on an occlusive narrative of Anglo-Irish relations conducted over many centuries, may account for the difficulty nationalist Ireland has had in coming fully to terms with the complexity of the social reality which is identified by the term British Ireland. Nationalist Ireland, accordingly, finds it almost impossible to recognise, to bring fully to public consciousness or perhaps to admit, how much of its current experience is defined not simply by England, but by the geography, economy and demography of these islands and by the processes of the British state, benign and malign, as the nationalist mind-set customarily finds the idea of an Irish person readily identifying himself or herself as British an evident absurdity. For the nationalist is marching to a different drum, to a tune that owes much to the idea of England as colonial oppressor and almost nothing to the idea of Britain as a complex and changing state. The British Irishman or woman hears that music and reckons it discordant and somehow alien to his or her ears. The notes that do rouse British Ireland's spirits are, in the nature of the case I have diagnosed, almost inaudible to nationalist Ireland.

That this is so was revealed, I think, in a very unsatisfactory series of paragraphs in the *New Ireland Forum* report of 1984. That document, which paved the way for the negotiations which bore fruit in the unfortunately named Anglo-Irish Agreement, was undoubtedly an earnest attempt to comprehend what it called 'the unionist point of view'. Paragraph 4.9 recorded that the Forum sought to abstract from the contributions of unionist participants 'What is it that the unionists wish to preserve?' Three elements, as the Report records were identified in their replies: 1) Britishness; 2) Protestantism; 3) The economic advantages of the British link. Setting aside the separation between Britishness and Protestantism, it is instructive to ponder the Report's gloss in paragraph 4.9.1 on 'Britishness'. It can best be described as platitudinous: 'Unionists generally regard themselves as being British, the inheritors of a specific communal loyalty to the British Crown. The traditional nationalist opposition to British rule is thus seen by unionists as incompatible with the survival of their sense of identity.'

But what may seem merely platitudinous, a statement of the obvious, in fact disguises a number of crucial misunderstandings about, and a lack of historical awareness of, the development of the Unionist community's idea of itself in this century. What is confused here is the Unionist sense of identity with the Unionist sense of loyalty. The Unionist is loyal to the British crown as the symbolic expression of the constitutional reality of the British state in whose commonwealth the citizen and subject feels his or her interests are most likely to be protected. His or her identity is a different matter. And a rather confused matter it is. He or she may have a sense of English or Scottish antecedents, but he or she cannot feel, living as they do on the island of Ireland to which their ancestors came centuries before, either English or Scottish. They resent accordingly, or did in the fairly recent past, the hijacking of what they believe a perfectly tenable idea – the idea of

Irishness, broadly defined, within the former United Kingdom of Great Britain and Ireland, and within the more recent United Kingdom of Great Britain and Northern Ireland – by a narrow, largely Catholic and aggressively Gaelic version of Irish identity. Early in the history of the two legislative units on this island, which remain the source of so much contention, it was not uncommon indeed for Unionist and loyalist spokespersons to decry the way in which the Irish Ireland project was appropriating, in an exclusive way, the idea of Irish identity to which the Unionist felt perfectly entitled. For example, the *Northern Whig* editorialised in 1925:

> When Ulster declined to join the South in separating from Great Britain it did not surrender its title as part of Ireland, nor renounce its share in those Irish traditions in art, in learning, in arms, in song, in sport and in science that were worth preserving in a united form.

And, as Dennis Kennedy has shown, in his useful study *The Widening Gulf: Northern attitudes to the independent Irish state, 1919–49,* Northern Unionists in the early period of Irish independence 'raised no objections to the continued use of "Ireland" and "Irish" to designate their churches, their sporting organisations and international teams and even the congress to which their trade unions belonged'. So little, indeed, did they object to the continued public expressions that their province was an Irish one, that an Englishman's suggestion of 1935 that Northern Ireland should more properly be termed 'North West Britain' was only put forward in the knowledge that it might be thought 'absurd' or 'almost mad'.

It was, in fact, as Irish Ireland's narrow view of Irish identity became entrenched in the new Irish state, and as that state legitimised a kind of irridentism in its 1937 constitution, that the notion that Ulster was British gained any real currency. It is this fact that gives a certain poignancy to the rest of paragraph 4.9.1 of the Forum Report which I have already cited, where, having reckoned that 'Unionists regard themselves as being British', the report continues: 'Unionists generally regard themselves as being Irish even if this does not include a willingness to live under all-Ireland political institutions. However, many of them identify with Ireland and with various features of Irish life, and their culture and way of life embrace much that is common to people throughout Ireland'. This seems a poignant statement in its bland failure to take account of the ways in which the term 'Irish' has been invested in this century with specific and exclusive meanings, and how the Unionists' wish to identify with 'various features of Irish life' has been significantly reduced by their sense that nationalist Ireland has a social and cultural project in hand which would take little account of their sensibilities and sense of themselves. Accordingly, in such a context, they saw, until fairly recently, no problem about taking an interest in their own traditions while proudly enjoying British citizenship.

Perhaps I may offer some autobiographical data at this point. My father was born in Belfast in 1911, in Snugville Street, off the Shankill Road in the heartland of the loyalist working-class city centre. His birth was registered by the attending mid-wife (a Margaret Redmond, a name to conjure with) who could not sign her own name but who appended her mark. My father was named Henry Montgomery, probably in honour not of the liberal opponent of Henry Cooke, but of an evangelical preacher more in Cooke's tradition than Montgomery's. Presbyterian, dissenting, working class (the birth certificate gives my grandfather's profession as 'mechanic'; I never knew him; he died while my father was still a child), evangelical, my father's social formation was, in the industrial city of Belfast, quintessentially 'British', in that any number of cities in the northern parts of these islands could have supplied comparisons. But Harry Brown was educated in a national school which had no doubts that Belfast was in Ireland. I remember his knowledge of Irish geography with envy – he could recite with pride (having learned by rote, in the manner of the times) the counties, rivers, towns, mountains of Ireland, and was properly concerned that my preparatory school education of the 1950's offered me no national perspectives whatsoever. On the contrary, I belong to that Northern Irish Protestant generation whose education was almost entirely English, with scarcely any Irish history, geography, literature or mythology laid down in childhood as a resource for adult negotiations of Irish social and cultural life. It did offer, however, a sense of the high cultural prestige of Science and Medicine – and not just as sound career options, but as vital modes of public service. In some sense we were given to understand that these fields were an aspect of the Ulster Protestant inheritance; the Law and the Arts were to some degree suspect (Catholics tended to make their way through the Arts and Law faculties at Queen's University).

The contrast between the two generations, my father's and my own, is striking – the one for whom Ireland was an undeniable hinterland to an urban British upbringing, the next a generation encouraged to consider itself British, with a fairly detailed knowledge of English history, but almost without consciousness that Ireland existed at all. As a consequence, the northern Protestant of my generation, and I am sure recent changes have not altered things very greatly, has no ready access to an Irish identity of any very developed kind. For the only one available, the Irish Ireland version of Irish identity and its rather unconsciously expressed nationalist descendent, even with goodwill on both sides, will inevitably often seem to such as myself, sectarian, self-righteous, exclusive, encoded with all sorts of political, cultural and racial assumptions that must be acceded to without demur. Even when Down plays at Croke Park we will, at half time, be affronted by the Furey brothers, in a tacky piece of racial propaganda, informing us in the doggerel of a bar-room ballad that 'The spirit of the Gael is in our games' and that 'North, south, east and west/Gaelic games are still the best'. We will always sense on such occasions, when enjoyment is never entirely innocent, that we are being asked to admit that our ancestors were on the wrong side in Irish history and that we can only be accepted as we recognise the error of their ways (my maternal grandfather signed the Ulster Covenant in 1912 and I can't bring myself to believe that he, a man whose living was the linen trade, acted only irrationally in opposing the protectionist economic policies of the Home Rule movement). And nationalism's traditional iconography, from Cuchulain to the profile of Pearse, from the mass rock to the Papal cross in the Phoenix Park which marks what the *Irish Press* in 1979 called 'a great hosting of the Gael', will similarly seem markedly alien, the properties of an Irish identity which in your guts you know you can't totally share since they were not unself-consciously yours in childhood, when personal identity was most profoundly influenced.

What, in summary, this brief excursion into autobiography, suggests is that in two generations, concurrently with the elevation of the Irish Ireland project to a role as the official ideology of the southern Irish state, northern Unionists were implementing an educational policy which cut off their people from even that overarching sense of an Irish identity which could find expression in the British context and which had characterised them at the time of Partition. It would be my hunch that Unionists now possess little sense of their Irishness (as, locally, Irish Ireland seems alive and well in aggressive form in the cultural policies of Sinn Féin, which could hardly commend it to Unionists) and a diminished respect for the Britishness they were recently happy to espouse, as the neighbouring island becomes a multi-ethnic society, apparently remote from their experience, and as the British government and the English people seem less and less inclined to include them in the British federation. Many educated young Ulstermen and women from Unionist homes these days, who in the past would have attended Queen's University, Belfast or even Trinity College, Dublin, seek therefore to leave Ireland altogether, to become properly British through attendance at British universities and employment on the 'mainland'. Better be fully British in Edinburgh or London, than half British and half nothing in Belfast.

If then, northern Unionists since the foundation of the southern Irish state have increasingly lost or abandoned their sense of being Irish, without discovering a secure British identity, in the last twenty to thirty years the southern part of the country has undergone a slow sea-change which involves the nationalist population of the country as a whole in a considerable crisis. I believe that in that period it has become evident to most people who are concerned about the matter that the Irish Ireland project, which began with Douglas Hyde's famous lecture of 1892 'On the Necessity of De-anglicising Ireland', has failed. Most crucially, the Irish language, central to the project will not now be revived as a vernacular of any numerically significant proportion of the Irish population. And without the Irish language the whole concept of Gaelic Ireland becomes attenuated and insecure. I think it was this unspoken recognition which, in part, accounted in 1980 for the widely sensed pertinence of Brian Friel's play *Translations* with its stark, poignant dramatisation of the inevitability of language-shift and its recognition that 'a civilisation can be imprisoned in a linguistic contour which no longer matches the landscape . . . of fact'. Irish, to be sure, remains and will remain as a resource for the creative imagination, a vital constituent of the life of small groups of committed individuals and local communities, a focus of dissentient radicalism, a humanistic resource and as a symbolic expression of the nation's sense of itself, rightly employed on official occasions. But it seems indisputable to me that for the great majority of citizens W.B. Yeats's famous formulation will increasingly have the ring of personal, regretful truth: 'Irish is my native language but it is not my mother tongue'.

The diminution of the significance of Gaelic Ireland in actual social life in a predominately Anglicised country has had curious, scarcely admitted, effects in the Republic of Ireland in the last two decades. One effect that I would identify has been a rather febrile attempt to repatriate writers and artists who, until quite recent times, were scarcely granted any attention whatsoever by the official mind (beyond, that is, the banning of their books). There has been a cranking up of the engine of a culture industry. Joyce and Beckett, for example, have been recruited to the Irishry in a way that would have been unthinkable even twenty years ago. They are now 'part of what we are', given official recognition, along with many of their successors who seem collectively to be required to go cultural bail for the nation. Which is not to deny the vitality of the artistic scene at present, especially in the regions, nor to ignore a vibrant, self-confident youth culture in which traditional music and rock each contribute to a sense of exuberant energy finding expression. But there is sometimes in the constant low-level cultural babble about our contemporary writers and dramatists and about the writers of the past (on the radio, on television and in the press), in the opportunistic commercialisation of high culture in tourism and summer school and literary competition, a sense of a nation insecurely adjusting to a state of perceived cultural loss and indigence. What are we if we don't have a distinctive culture but an economically under-developed, sadly inefficient market for ideas, goods, services and cultural products from Britain and the United States? So a distinctive culture we must have and our writers must supply it, even if the demand ignores in many instances how 'Irish' writers cannot easily be corralled by that restrictive national designation and how many of them express in their work a profound alienation from past and present Irish realities. Commerce is permitted to intrude upon civic and imaginative space in the sponsorship of kitsch versions of artistic achievement in the nation's capital. Ireland is offered as a set for international cinematography at the expense of an embryonic local film industry.

The subversive energies of such as Joyce and Beckett are rendered anodyne as they are assimilated to marketable notions of Dublin as a European cultural capital. They are recruited as Parisians and artists of European reputation to help give credibility to a further current self-understanding. That is the often bruited idea of Ireland as a European nation. Now as Professor O Tuathaigh has suggested this morning, this idea has a degree both of authenticity and of social utility. Nevertheless, I cannot help suspecting that sometimes the attempt to deem Ireland a European country owes more to an effort to assert national distinctiveness than to real understanding of the European experience. If we can't be Gaelic we can at least be European and, accordingly, different from the inhabitants of the neighbouring island who lack that quality. In his play *Translations* Friel has Hugh, the hedge-school master, profess ignorance of Wordsworth and aver to the English Lieutenant Yolland: 'I'm afraid we're not familiar with your literature, Lieutenant. We feel closer to the warm Mediterranean. We tend to overlook your island'. This is to give expression to a view which has been quite widely disseminated recently by members of the country's nationalist intelligentsia. It is fairly frequently argued these days that Ireland is somehow more European and cosmopolitan in outlook and orientation than the sadly provincial England: an idea that depends for its rhetorical force on a view of England that bears little detailed inspection (English intellectual life has been deeply implicated in, and has contributed to, European thought for at least two centuries) and ignores how Britain also includes Scotland with its own distinctive European traditions of Calvinism, Enlightenment and nationalism. But it is also I suspect a coded way of dismissing from consciousness how comprehensively Ireland has been Anglicised in this century. The fact, depressing indeed from the nationalist point of view, can be suppressed in an attempt to overlook the neighbouring island's complex history and present: an attempt which exaggerates the current Irish links with European intellectual life, while downgrading or ignoring those with Britain.

What I suspect is the altogether less dramatic truth of the matter, which those indulging in this cultural form of wish-fulfilment find difficult to admit, is that in recent times England has been somewhat less European in its cultural concerns than in the past (but it is only recently that English poetry's long romance with Italy seems to have come to an end), while Ireland has been slightly more attentive to European developments than in the immediate past (in the thirties, of course, it was European corporatism that seemed *le dernier cri* to elements of the intelligentsia, the way deconstruction and post-moderism do now). And perhaps the historian of the future will be more impressed, as he or she considers the Europeanisation of these islands in the late twentieth century, by the fact that in the early 1990's the south of England and the European continent were connected by a channel tunnel, bringing London, Paris, Antwerp and Brussels into a new kind of proximity, than by the hesitant cosmopolitanism of Irish culture in the same period.

Which brings us back to British Ireland. An event as definitive as the opening of the channel tunnel, ending millennia of insular life on the landmass of Britain, is the kind of thing which should surely concentrate Irish minds on the fact that the destiny of the Irish nation, whatever its European future, must be worked out in the context of what, for want of a better term, must be called the British Isles. (We badly need an alternative name – 'these islands' is a fudge). For I believe that the events of 1989, and the re-emergence of central and eastern European nationalism in the last few years, have probably postponed movement towards European integration (we hear less and less of 1992 as it encroaches in reality) and, accordingly, greater attention must be directed to comprehension of our position, politically, socially and culturally as Unionists and Nationalists in the wider context of the history of the British Isles in a rapidly changing Europe. Writing recently, the historian Hugh Kearney has compared these islands to the valley of the Danube, the Iberian or Italian peninsula, considering them as an area 'in which various cultures struggled for supremacy or survival over a thousand years or more'. He writes in the conclusion to his book *The British Isles*:

> During the crisis of the Great War . . . the English empire of the British Isles did not break up as completely as the Habsburg empire. It did, however, suffer a deep wound, when the Irish Free State was established in 1922. In due course, after the Second World War during which Eire remained neutral, the Republic of Ireland was established (1949). Other ethnic divisions within the United Kingdom led to demands for political independence but when it came to the test of a plebiscite in the late 1970s, the political and cultural balance of power remained unaltered. During the 1980s, however, it was possible to discern a shift of population and wealth to the south-east and a growing centralisation based upon London . . . Writing in 1990, however, there is no sign that the British Isles is ceasing to be an

enduring historical unit, of which the Republic of Ireland forms
part, and to which new, non-European ethnic groups are now
making a contribution.

As the century ends, and as in Ireland the attempt to build a
distinctive Gaelic identity in the South peters out and the reactive
attempt to build an almost entirely political British identity in the
Unionist North results in cultural incoherence and political impo-
tence, it is I believe imperative that, North and South, we begin to
examine honestly and openly the nature of our involvement with
the neighbouring island of Britain. This I consider an imperative
for national health: for a society and a culture which assiduously
ignores or suppresses central facts about its existence is open to
enfeebling self-delusions and consequent exploitation. But, as we
come more fully to terms with our actual states of being, so we may
the better be able to reckon with our relationship with each other
on this island as well. In this process Unionists must surely come to
terms with the fact that they belong to no other nation but the
Irish. But this exercise of self-discovery would, perhaps, uncover to
what degree and in what varying ways the idea of a British Ireland
can be an enabling one for everyone living in Ireland. And by this
term I now mean an Ireland that must work out its complex
destiny in the context of the inter-relationships of all the peoples
of the offshore islands of Europe who share a language, an economy
dominated by that of the south of England, and a profoundly
entangled history.
   And I expect it might be enabling not only to the inhabitants of
Ireland but to our neighbours in Britain who can surely learn
from us as we from them. For far too long Britain has only
perceived Ireland as a colonial opportunity, then a problem and
then a burdensome duty. It's time Britain was made aware of
Ireland's contribution to its own life and the human and cultural
resource it represents as in the new Europe, now in the making in
the wake of cataclysmic continental events, we redefine all our
relationships. We in the Republic of Ireland are the only society in
this part of the world which has had experience of living with a
written constitution, a matter surely of interest to Charter 88. We
have also had the experience of moving from monarchy to a
republican form of government, a matter surely of interest to
Scottish nationalists. We have a national church which is not
formally a state church, though the implications of that fraught

relationship have not yet all been satisfactorily confronted. Nevertheless, at least we have begun the process of disentanglement. But we can scarcely expect Britain to be aware of what we might have to offer its societies when we ourselves suppress awareness of our 'British' context so comprehensively. Some questions are worth asking as a means to inaugurating a discussion of these and related matters. Among these perhaps are:

1. What has been the Irish experience, benign and malign, in Britain since partition? We know there is such an entity as Irish America. Does such a thing as Irish Britain have meaning and if so what might it be? Why has there been so little study of this question, even though an Irish population of about a third of that living in the Republic of Ireland currently lives in Britain? How can we encourage educational authorities in Britain to pay more attention to Irish experience in Britain and in Ireland?

2. What is the nature of Anglicisation in Ireland? Is it regionally distinctive? Does its degree vary regionally and in terms of class? And are there regions of Britain and Ireland which have common interests which might be the basis of comparative study and the sharing of expertise?

   Are there regions of Ireland which have historic socio/cultural links with regions of Britain and *vice versa*?
   If there are, how might these be developed?

3. How might an increased awareness of, and sensitivity to, the complex inter-relationship of the four nations on these islands contribute to our capacity to deal with the most difficult of our current Irish and British challenges: the need to reach a peaceful, just and long-lasting resolution of the ongoing northern crisis?

PART III

CHAIRPERSONS' REPORTS FROM WORKSHOPS

BRITISH IRELAND/IRISH IRELAND

Chairman:
I think it is right I should draw attention to the fact that, during the luncheon adjournment, I was informed by Mary Holland that the 2000th civilian has been killed in Northern Ireland. I mention this because one of the things that I have been seeking to impress, although it is hardly necessary to impress on this audience, is the urgency of what we are about.

I would now ask the Chairpersons of the various workshops to make their reports: Professor Anthony Clare, Professor Edna Longley, Mr Justice Niall McCarthy and Dr Margaret MacCurtain.

WORKSHOP 1: British Ireland

Anthony Clare:
I think the easiest way to do this is under the three headings we adopted – broad areas we discussed, the developments we discussed, and recommendations. You will know from your own programme that the areas to be discussed were pretty broad to begin with: the nature and extent of the cultural influences arising from Britain on the Republic of Ireland – Are they regional or class related? – Can they be used and adapted positively and creatively? How they can help us relate within this island with its division and diffusion and disparity? What have the Irish in Britain to tell us and can we hear them? And two later questions: about whether in fact that was all too narrow – the notion of Europe, together with a certain gourmet's paradise at the end. Which bits will we take from the menu of Britain/Ireland and which will we leave on the plate? [**See pp. 106–7 for workshop questions.**]

Well, it will not surprise any of you to know that one of the very first contributions pointed out to us that even the notion of

Anglicisation is very narrow. Tom Kilroy said that his influences through the English language extend to the Caribbean and Nigeria, as well as of course to more obvious places – North America, Australasia. That stunned us temporarily into a humble recognition that these are large issues. Then we wrestled with the exposure in Ireland to British media – newspapers and television. In this discussion I think the group oscillated between feeling a certain confidence about the resilience of Ireland, North and South, to sustain a native culture: an Irish culture, literary, musical, artistic was much emphasised. It depended whether you felt the transformation of Madonna into Van Morrison reflected cultural strength or a passing phenomenon. In time, as these young people became our age, the discos, the bands, the vitality, the music, the transformation might sadly not produce political, educational, cultural and religious alterations of lasting impact, in terms of the problems we face.

The discussion also focussed on the extent to which we might, using education, and the media, alter or influence or examine further the state of play. Because, as the discussion developed towards its latter part, it became clear that we needed so much more information. You can understand from the discussion last night and various rebukes, that this was one workshop that was intent on being practical, hardheaded, eschewing psychological speculation. Certainly, I think the Chairman will be relieved to know, that there was precious little in the way of psycho-analytic expressions of personal angst, but nonetheless we did find that perhaps one of the reasons we were treated to such situations in addition to being treated to deviant psychiatrists who have nothing better to do, is that we lack a lot of information and data, and perhaps this was never truer than when we came to two groups, the Irish in Britain and the young Irish in Ireland – North and South.

The recommendations? An early recommendation, of such stunning clarity that it actually led to very little discussion, was that the Irish in Britain should be enfranchised here. I think it was implicit in all the discussion that followed, that this was both a symbolic and practical acknowledgement, an element so missing in terms of its political voice, that our knowledge of them, our interest in them, was much reduced. We had no need in one sense to take account of them. There were various reasons also why we might prefer not to. As indeed, why they might prefer us not to, in so far

as attitudes towards us could be discerned from our discussion
group, so mixed are they and separated from us in a largely
political way. Nonetheless, that was our first recommendation.

The second arose from a contribution that James Hawthorne
made at the very outset, which concerned the fact, not known to
all of us, that Ireland, as part of the world community, has been
given a satellite footprint. This means we have access, albeit costly,
to a bit of a satellite in the sky which can broadcast to an area, a
footprint, which, doesn't quite approximate, but damn precious
close to it, to an archipelago (as we are increasingly calling it, I
notice), of Britain, and Ireland – forty-five million people or
thereabouts.

This interested me, because one of the constant complaints
about the impact of British culture on us is that it is all one way. We
read their newspapers, we watch their television and we follow
their footballers. But, as certainly those of us who have lived there
know, they don't read our newspapers, they don't watch our
television, except in very rare circumstances, and they just raid our
footballers. Now, the problem, James Hawthorne quickly reminded
us, and here you'll see the dangers ahead unless we quickly start
the discussion rolling, is that it is costly. One way in which the Irish
response to this satellite footprint could express itself is that we
could just 'flog it off', in his elegant term. That's to say, it's a large
sum of money, someone else would buy it off us. And in our name,
or not in our name at all as I understand it from him, it would
transmit to this large population.

Now, as he pointed out over lunch, it is difficult to see how
Ireland could manage this satellite on its own – it's very costly.
But it does seem to us an area where, if we wished, this complex
culture might express itself to our neighbouring island in such a
way that they would at least begin to comprehend to a greater
extent the complexity here, and the relationships between the
two islands. Obviously, modern technology has afforded the possibility.

Our next recommendation? It became clear in the discussion
that we tend to discuss culture narrowly – historians are here,
novelists are here, poets are here, academics are here – but science doesn't figure too largely. Nor does technology. A perceptive
analyst in our group had noted that the marketing of some
upmarket products on Irish radio and television is accompanied
by an accent of a very superior and identifiably well cultured

kind, whereas other products are marketed with very different kinds of accents – all subtly reinforcing certain aspects of our own culture in ways that perhaps we haven't sufficiently reflected upon. Now this in turn led to a discussion about the role of advertising in the shaping of a culture – in reflecting a culture. And surely, at some future date, in some future forum, if we are going to be discussing the future of Ireland, that input must be there. These advertising people are tapping elements of what is commonly called culture, for a variety of hard-headed business reasons. They can give us cultural information, but we also need to watch them.

So the recommendation is that a future forum might well broaden its membership in a variety of ways. There have been other discussions about other ways, but in this instance we focussed upon how to broaden the terms of 'culture' – the definition of the nature of culture. Another recommendation emerged from a discussion about the constitution. There are two constitutional ideals: the constitutional demand for unification, and the constitutional position of the Irish language. Maurice Hayes was one of a number who pointed out that in a sense these ideals could be seen as antithetical. What we need, if indeed there is to be a constitutional review and reform and a new constitution, is a statement which clearly, authoritatively and emphatically asserts the status, the worth and the qualities of both languages – English and Irish – in the Irish domain.

It was clear, when we were concentrating on this issue of the Irish in Britain, that we need still more than what has already been set in place. I'm thinking of the British Association for Irish Studies, which has led to a variety of gains which I may in turn refer to. But the feeling, nonetheless, was that this was only a start. We need an impetus. There was particular emphasis on the need for an impetus in relation to young people. We were conscious time and again, partly perhaps to reassure ourselves, that the vigour of our culture could be seen in the evidence of our young people. They did this, or that, or the other. But they aren't here, and some of us anecdotally recorded that on their being asked to be at something like this, we got diverse answers that reflected unclearly as to quite what their position about Irish culture might be. So we suggest another and deliberate effort to involve young people – from both sides of the border –   in a discussion, in an exchange, in a dynamic concerning issues such as we have discussed this weekend. A number of people from Northern Ireland were interested in having young people interrogate, I think was the word, people who are in prominent positions in shaping the culture of Northern Ireland and of the Republic of Ireland. But we didn't, because of the nature of the discussion, spend much time on how this might be done. It was an aspirational recommendation, rather than a detailed one.

But there were some detailed recommendations about education. We felt that that the Education for Mutual Understanding development in Northern Ireland could be introduced here, into our schools. It could be extended not merely to include an analysis aimed at improving and understanding the relations within this island, but indeed, again to use the word, within the archipelago. It should be expanded in Northern Ireland, introduced here, and then comes the thorny issue of how to develop further the educational exposure in Britain to Irish issues. The 'A' Level in Irish studies is a gain, a very definite gain and a credit to the British Association for Irish Studies, and a beginning. However, there is a tendency to think of such recommendations as we could make in terms of third-level education. But we should not baulk perhaps, given the size of the Irish community in Britain, at exploring opportunities of introducing Irish studies at an earlier level in the British educational system. But, of course, that would be influenced by the other changes going on in that system at the present time.

It is always dangerous summing up what was an extremely animated, clear discussion. But you can see the key themes in the recommendations. A desire for the broadening of the issue of culture. A desire for a greater degree of information about what is actually happening. Certainly some hard-headed recommendations about getting in on the discussion about what the Irish satellite is going to be doing, and who is going to use it and who is going to affect some of the issues we have described. Some very hard-headed, although difficult to implement, educational recommendations geared to improving the visibility of Ireland-in-Britain in Ireland. Bearing in mind the grim news we have just heard, we must always have the clear aim of improving the understanding of those people who live within this island and are wrestling with the issues. What Gearóid O'Tuathaigh and Terence Brown said so eloquently this morning, opened them up for us.

WORKSHOP 2: British Ireland

Edna Longley:
Following on from Anthony Clare, I began by suggesting that a psychiatric model had been present in our conference discussions, that the term repression had been used (and went on being used in our workshop), in the sense that cultural dimensions had been repressed North and South after 1921. I also mentioned at the beginning that I had noticed some concern on various fronts for cultural particularities in Ireland, and the idea of fostering those and protecting them in an enriching and open way. This seemed common ground. And the third point I made was the need for concrete proposals to come from this conference.

Our first speaker indicated a failure to reflect on the ways in which British culture is mediated in Ireland – what are the media of transmission? Are people in the Republic reflective enough about a silent Britishness, and if they were more conscious and articulate on this matter might it be a more positive force? Gearóid O'Tuathaigh then raised the awkward question of where does acknowledgement of a British dimension become capitulation, a capitulation which is painful? The Irish football team was once again mentioned in this connection, one speaker claiming that the delight in its success proved the acceptance of that British dimension. Somebody else pointed out that they were not celebrated as British, in their British cultural permutations, but as an instance of Irish success. I recalled that I had heard Brendan MacLua – proprietor of the *Irish Post* – a man with whose opinions I would normally not agree, say very angrily: 'It wasn't the Irish football team that did well in the World Cup, the *Irish in Britain* did well in the World Cup'. I think that bears out what Anthony Clare has been saying.

One member of the group suggested that there were five nations in the archipelago – that the Ulster Unionists had an equally valid argument for terming themselves a nation. Then, at various points we covered the issue of whether discussion in Republic, or debate in the Republic about diversity, should be entirely for the sake of the Republic. There was the argument that it would happen anyway as part of internal development. It shouldn't be undertaken to impress the North or impress Unionists. But this may turn out to be a complex matter, because the Unionist present indicated that he would have been impressed if, at the point where choices were made in the referenda, the Republic had made a statement about itself in pluralistic terms. Someone else maintained that there *is* an anxiety and concern about the North and the vocabulary and imagery of the state are very much implicated in the Northern question. There is a need, perhaps, to change that vocabulary. I noted the tendency for debate in the Republic to become unduly self-enclosed, and indeed this happened in our own session once the referenda were mentioned. We were talking about church and state in the Republic and any sense that there might be some Northern input into that didn't seem to apply. Nor did the question of whether the Southern debate had affected the Roman Catholic church in the North. Issues like that weren't raised. I mention this because it's a very delicate balancing act that might need to go on in different contexts, and in terms of their mutual awareness, as South and North explore their internal diversity and what that means for their relations with each other or with the other island.

John Wilson Foster asked: was there any point in a homogenous society like the Republic having such a debate with itself about diversity? He instanced Canada as a place where multi-culturalism, which in a sense was coming apart at the seams, was nonetheless a logical move: just as in Northern Ireland multi-culturalism, or some cultural exploration, could cut across a rigid binary notion of culture in the North that was clearly unreal as well as dangerous. It was suggested that maybe the Republic exports its diversity and closes back in on itself. And once again we mentioned the Irish in Britain who went to Great Britain to a multi-cultural society, and came back to Ireland, or didn't. Their multi-culturalism becomes a generational thing, and we asked what their 'home' island had actually to say in terms of diversity to its diverse emigrant populations.

Another speaker mentioned the need for voiceless people to have some impact on the shape of culture, and it was said that the shapers and thinkers were not necessarily all to be found in the middle class. It was suggested, indeed, that working-class people were more at ease with the cultural exports from Britain than the élites in the Republic, who had some difficulty about 'high culture' being connected with 'big house' antecedents – and had hang-ups in that direction. Perhaps that fits in with what Terence Brown said about Europeanism this morning.

There was an argument about whether there was a predominantly Catholic ethos still in the schools in the Republic. That was a very fierce argument, and somebody from the North pointed out that the fact that this argument was taking place, in the terms that it was, was a sign of change. And there was an impression from Northerners that society was both changing and, paradoxically, remaining conservative. This conservatism had to do, perhaps, with the failure of thinkers (again not all from the middle class) to influence politicians, civil servants. There seemed a reluctance to give any kind of lead or formulate policies which reflected social and cultural actualities. Somebody said that public institutions were very out of kilter with private behaviour, private actualities. There was a big failure to admit this in the public domain, and to take responsibility for action which would bring institutions more into line with what is actually happening in the society.

The group regarded this assumption of responsibility as the overall necessity. I'll briefly list the more concrete proposals.

Local studies, as in the Northern context, came up as an important means of fostering more diverse pictures of history. Gordon Lucy pointed out that here we are in Dun Laoghaire-stroke-Kingstown, and he had opened a local history pamphlet which said nothing of the Unionist past of this neck of the woods. Again, that's something that shouldn't simply be thrown out the window as if it never happened – there should at least be some focus for awareness and discussion.

There was general approval for trying to influence the curriculum in the way in which it was developing in the North, although there's still a lot of work to be done in the North. EMU and Cultural Heritage should be on the agenda for educational reform in the Republic. It was pointed out that school teachers need time and resources if curricula are to change and that's expensive, and in the North not enough attention has been given to this. School teachers are expected to do too much too quickly without sufficient support, and proper backing would be necessary in the Republic also.

Several of us with some experience of Cultural Heritage in the North suggested that as an intellectual enterprise it was a good thing anyway, whether or not any results in the short term came out of it. There had been an inert curriculum which didn't pay any attention to the local particularities of the North-east and indeed its relation to the rest of Ireland and Great Britain, and the shift was exciting and had a lot of potential. But again, sufficient resources and sufficient commitment must be put into it, because the point was also made that this was a substitute for integrated education, and an evasion of integrated education. If that's the way it is to be done, it has to be done seriously.

English influences came up, as did the point that there's comparatively little cultural information coming from Scotland and Wales. We echoed Terence Brown's question: 'Why is the Republic not exploring links with Scotland and Wales in cultural and other areas?'. Then finally, as with Anthony Clare's workshop, we wanted much more support for the British Association for Irish Studies. Again, money and resources are needed for its progress and possibilities and what it might mean to the Irish in Britain and to the British in Ireland, if that was to be followed through.

WORKSHOP 3: Irish Ireland

Justice Niall McCarthy:

Mr Chairman, our workshop was structured on a basis that everyone would have a say and no-one would have the power of contradiction until everyone had had a say. In a way it suffered from the diktat that I imposed at the start in a bid to give fair play to everybody.

Nonetheless, I think it has performed a useful function. I might mention in opening, having reproved someone for the use of anecdotage, I proceeded to do so myself, quite naturally, by referring to Terence Brown's emotional reference to the mail boat – which I see has just gone out again. Having been reared down the road, and having gone to school across the road, it was particularly evocative to me – the reference to the mail boat going out – because for the first time it dawned on me the significance it had for my childhood that the waves it emitted, so to speak, used to hit Seapoint sixteen minutes after it went out through the harbour mouth. And this, by proper timing, enabled us to ride to those waves, both initially physically and later mentally or metaphorically.

We didn't pay much attention to the terms of reference I'm afraid, and that wasn't from any lack of intent. But rather we got off to a stumble of a start on the basis that there was an imbalance in the structure of the attendance at the conference itself, the workshop itself. We had few dissenters in the real sense – there was a kind of unhappy consensus virtually. We had no murderers, or representatives of murderers, and that was regarded as rather unfortunate. The consensus I think certainly – you will have to accept that it's my reading of the consensus rather than necessarily what the consensus was – maintained that it would be a good thing to enter into dialectic or into debate with those who represent the men and women of violence in Northern Ireland – that no debate can be of any value until that happens.

Secondly, tribute was particularly paid to the almost startling, in an Irish political context, observations of the Minister of State last night, when he said: 'The politicians and ministers must adapt to new ways of speaking'. Mr Flood perhaps opened a door greater than many of us had ever contemplated could be done in Irish political life because of what he said.

Their further recommendation in this regard, was that we must translate what is being said into a language which is understood by all. Now this is a very major problem which was exemplified by reference even to certain words. What does Gospel mean either in the South of Ireland or in the North or even between the two? We know what the Church means, in the South. What does it mean in the North? But, more particularly, what do so many differences of words and different nuances of language have as their common meaning? What we are saying ourselves to our friends, to our relations must be translated. It must be understood by the dissenters, of whom there are none spectacularly here. It must be understood by the young, of whom there are none here. The comment was made that we have here the generations of the Fifties and Sixties, but we haven't many of the Seventies generation. The comment was also made that young people are no longer tied to the type of influences that formed most of us. The views of more than 50% of the population are not being heard at all here – save in so far as they can be through their parents or through their relations.

Much emphasis was laid on the importance of a proliferation of discussion groups, examples being given from Northern Ireland where there are many. Indeed there are many examples of groups involved in discussion about the future, not in discussion about the past. It was of immense importance that the discussion of cultural needs in those groups should go beyond an either/or proposition. It must go forwards in finding a better proposition; otherwise one is only perpetuating the division.

There were comments on the decline of church influence, in the sense of the Church as we understand it in the Republic. But the lack of radical dissent in Catholic and Protestant circles appears to be undergoing a change. Radical dissent has come back.

It was said that it may lead to a convergence on what was dramatically referred to last night by Margaret MacCurtain as the demolition of the Catholic monolith, which she waits to experience.

Incidentally, it was quite apparent that our debate, our discussion, our observations, our statements and positions were personal-experience related. It seems virtually impossible in an Irish context to introduce an objectivity. I suppose everyone has their own necessities reduced to objectivities on some topic, but on an Irish topic Irish people are singularly unable to bring an objectivity to bear. Therefore we go back to the point that we should ask the young and be guided by the young.

It was noted, or was certainly to be interpreted, that the difference of approach between Catholic and Protestant was similar to the personal decision as against the magisterial diktat. I have a phrase for this: that it can be defined as the debate between populism and papalism – as a convenient mode of reference.

Finally I think it is fair to say that our comments went around the subject without coming to any specifically concrete suggestions, but rather to emphasise once more the importance of translating what is being said into a language which will be understood by all.

WORKSHOP 4: Irish Ireland

Margaret MacCurtain:
After an opening plenary discussion we narrowed down the agenda which we were asked to look at to two points.

We took up the points that Gearóid O'Tuathaigh made in the morning session, and also the realisation that there was actually a generation of people in the North who were cut off from an Irish heritage in one form or another. We needed to think about that particular generation, an in-between generation. And we kept coming back to the cut-off between different groupings in the country: Northern Catholics and Southern Catholics are not the same breed, nor have Northern Protestants and Southern Protestants the same identity. We wondered about Northern Nationalists and how they were different from Southern Nationalists. And we also wondered how Northern Unionists differed from the unionists who are still abroad in the South, so to speak.

Positive initiatives could arise from experiencing difference. Jennifer Johnston talked about the freshness of creative writing sessions in Northern schools and the potential of the EMU programme referred to by another speaker. Brenda from Galway spoke about the exchanges of womens' groups North and South, which are such a fascinating aspect of life in this island at the present moment.

The community and cultural awareness that should happen in the Republic must counteract sharply the kind of blandness and smugness that exist. Perhaps begin at school level. One of the aims of Co-Operation North is to interact at youth level. We felt that this was an important area that we would like to develop.

We were reminded, as Terence and Gearóid had reminded us, of the deep-seated political differences between Catholic and Protestant. There was consensus that Articles 2 and 3 of the constitution (in a sense they are legal fictions that must be tackled) should be removed. There are obstacles in the constitution that have to be confronted promptly.

We broke into five smaller groups and we reflected for about twenty minutes. We came back again and again to the realisation that we are a young country, and this conference really should be about youth. Co-Operation North and the model of the exchange groups we felt was an important reinforcement of something that has been successful as an initiative. There was a need to pass on optimism in our society.

There is a new identity around sport at the present time, but as well as that national focus there are symbolic kinds of cultural notions around sport – for example, the Down victory in the GAA – that we needed to look at, as well as the sometimes conflictual group identities built upon sport.

Group 4 again came back to the whole identity of Northern Nationalists and Southern Nationalists – this difference needs to be teased out. There are simple and complex notions of identity on these levels. There is the possible anchorage of identity in the language, and we would like to have spent more time on that, taking up Gearóid's point this morning – how central language is to this whole area. We were interested in particularity without exclusivity.

We must also think about the less-educated people on this island, particularly in Northern Ireland, but also in the Republic, who are the most likely to suffer harrassment and violence. There are areas of our cities that do not suffer or do not encounter the harrassment or violence which are problems that cross gender and sometimes even class.

The most urgent recommendation that we bring back to the floor was generated by Brian Lennon and Jennifer Johnston: the whole situation of university students at the present time. Why are they, with the mobility that they possess, moving away from the country? Why are the Northern university students who formerly came to Trinity or UCD now going to England? Why are a number of students from the Republic also going to England? What is that doing to an élite which is very, very important for the future of this country? So, much of our pondering reflected a concern that the educational needs of the young people in this country would be understood, would be identified and perhaps would be put forward in new initiatives through the appropriate channels.

GENERAL DISCUSSION

Chairman:
Thank you to all of the Chairpersons and their reporters and all the participants in the four workshops. Constance Short has asked me to say *à propos* of something that Justice McCarthy said, that various organisations were asked to attend, and either didn't respond or declined to attend. They included: Conradh Na Gaeilge, Comhaltas, Family Solidarity and Sinn Féin.

Now, nobody believes, of course, that the précis of the workshops can be comprehensive. They are necessarily the views of chairpersons and reporters about what was significant and what wasn't, and for that very reason I think it is very important at this stage to throw those reports open for discussion. It will necessarily have to be a fairly short discussion, so that if anyone thinks that there are glaring distortions or omissions, or that there are aspects of the subject that are totally untouched upon, now is the time to say so. Bearing always in mind that this necessarily is a beginning, and cannot be more than a beginning, but we must begin if we are to weave with the right set-up in our loom. So are there any threads missing – are there any themes that haven't been touched upon that people think should be touched upon, or are there serious distortions in any of the reports from the workshops in anyone's view?

John Waters (*Irish Times*):
I would be anxious that there was an emphasis in almost all of the workshops on the question of young people. I think that's a bit of a cliché in Irish life – I think it has been a cliché for a long time –

50% of our people are under 25 or whatever it is. That might be seen as simply patronising them in inviting them to be involved, or being concerned about their non-involvement. I think we should actually say very clearly that there is an urgent necessity first of all to make connections with the culture of young people. And this is linked with politics. We need to connect the thinking of young people with the thinking of the political process, and this is a question of leadership. That's where we are sadly lacking. The presidency has provided a guideline and a direction, but we need something more. And the only place that I can think of where this connection has been made is in Czechoslovakia with the presidency of Václav Havel, who has actually managed to tap into that feeling, that culture and express it in terms of a moral philosophy. I think one of the problems of this country is that there is dichotomy between the expression of a morality and behaviour, and that confuses young people and actually pulls them into a ghetto of culture which is not comprehended by outsiders, by older people. And I think we should look, not just to Britain or not just within ourselves, but at the political developments which are having a profound effect on the young people, who are conscious in a very real way of what is happening in the world. I was in the square in Prague last year after the revolution. Paul Simon, a rock star from America, was playing there, a very well-known rock star, very popular all over the world, and before he came on the announcer announced that the president was coming on.

Václav Havel stumbled on in these jeans and jumper and made a short speech of introduction to Paul Simon, and the whole town square in Prague was full of young people, and they were cheering and stomping and clapping, and they weren't at all interested in Paul Simon. They didn't want their President to leave and I think that's what we should aim for in this country.

Voice:
Give us a Václav Havel.

Brendan O'Regan (Co-Operation North):
Chairman, I would just like to make this point. Culture and economy are very much bound up. In Europe after two great world wars they said: 'We'll never let it happen again.' They defused hates and fears greater than anything we have ever had on this island, between the Germans and the French and the British, by eco-

nomic co-operation which they managed from Brussels. We have seen the results that has had in reaching a situation where it can never happen again in Europe. I would like to ask: 'What can this very important gathering of people who think very deeply about our problems do to ensure that we will learn from that lesson, and recognise that political change and political agreement follows economic co-operation and economic agreement. We must take steps to try and speed up the whole process of co-operation on this island between North and South and between the two Irelands.

[At this point a contributor referred to Ian Paisley as 'the leader of the largest political party in Northern Ireland'.]

Robin Wilson (editor of *Fortnight*):
I'm actually very disturbed by what was just said. One of the problems that I was made aware of by a couple of journalists from this side of the border who went to the recent media conference in Belfast, was their surprise at the extent to which even journalists in Belfast seemed to think that everything in the politics of the Republic focussed around, or ought to focus around, the political longevity of the Taoiseach. And they thought it was stunning – this superficiality, even amongst journalists, in terms of perceptions of the South: for example, lack of knowledge about the detail of Greencore, Telecom and all the current scandals. I'm equally appalled, therefore, by the tendency to refer to a very generalised notion of Paisleyism, when in fact the party has been in decline since 1981. But also, within the Protestant community Paisleyism is only one strand. It's those kinds of stereotyped images, on both sides of the border, which are a massive block on any kind of progress.

Voice:
But should they not be mentioned?

Robin Wilson:
Oh yes, they should be mentioned. But only in the context of the wider tapestry of which he is an unpleasant, unfortunate part.

Chairman:
Sorry, but before you leave that Robin, I think you are the person to whom one should ask this question. Why is there this blockage of communication?

Robin Wilson:

In terms of Southern perceptions of the North, as I said last night, I think it is hard to go past the sheer turn-off of the violence as a factor blotting it out of peoples' minds. And from a purely journalistic point of view, the problem of how you get anybody in the South to read about the North, when the North just means violence and the Provos. I was talking to the editor of a very distinguished Irish newspaper yesterday, who was saying to me: 'had I read the interview that Frank Millar did with Peter Brooke?'. He said: 'I suppose you read every word of it'. I said yes. He said: 'Well you are the only person in Ireland who did so' – although he did qualify that by saying there would be fifty people who would read it. In terms of the other side, in terms of Northern attitudes to the South, there is a genuine difficulty because of the integrity of the conflict in the North, the way it does encourage a very inward-looking perspective. It is a major barrier, because in lots of ways if only Unionists and Nationalists in the North were actually more aware of the reality of the 'new Ireland' that has been emerging over the last number of years South of the border, first of all it would encourage Northern Nationalists to think more self-critically about their own position; and it would, in particular, hopefully discourage the sense that so many Unionists have that the South is still the bogey that is out to get them.

Chairman:

Now, can I just be even more unfair Robin, while you are still there? What can we do? Clearly you believe it was worth coming – or you believed it was: after last night, I'm not sure you still believe it. But what further can we do? How can we break down these appalling barriers that are bedevilling the situation?

Robin Wilson:

John Waters mentioned the President. I was upbraided by some-one of a Unionist persuasion last night for referring to 'our President'. But I do think of our President as our President, and I do think that that is not untrue of a lot of people in Northern Ireland. It does seem to me that the phrase that Mary Robinson used in the campaign, and which has been subsequently trans-lated into reality, of 'extending the hand of friendship' with no ideological strings attached, is exactly the right approach. It has

done a tremendous amount to disarm and disable potential oppo-
nents of that kind of dialogue in the North, of which there are
plenty. It has been quite striking, the number of people who have
been coming down here from the North to the Aras – and that has
included on one occasion the chair of East Belfast Unionist Association. A very short time ago that would have led to his being
hounded into outer darkness.

Arthur Aughey (University of Ulster):
As the person of the Unionist persuasion who upbraided Robin, I
was doing so tongue-in-cheek. I personally believe that Mary
Robinson's election to the Presidency is one of the most hopeful
and significant developments in Irish politics, in my lifetime at any
rate. But I think the significant thing about this conference is that
it has exploded one particular myth, and that is that the only
people who have an identity crisis are Unionists. The atmosphere
of this conference suggests that one form of equality we have now
is that we all have an identity crisis. We have been trying to find
some kind of common ground on which to explore that crisis. And
I was asking myself, and reflecting on the reason why that might be
so for people in the Republic. It seems to me in terms of the
contributions that have been made, brilliant contributions in the
lectures today, and contributions from the floor and in the semi-
nars this morning, that the spirit of the Nationalist cultural project
of 1916 has died in the Republic. But the spirit of that cultural
project of 1916 is still alive in Northern Ireland. And I think part of
the reason for its being alive, in the murderous way in which it is
alive in some sections of the community of Northern Ireland, has
to do, to a degree, with the official doctrine of the Irish Republican state. And therefore I would support the various comments
that have been made about changes to Articles 2 and 3. I think that
would be one significant development. But Mary Holland has
consistently written about this problem and mentioned it to me
earlier on today; there are great difficulties (and I recognise this
even as a supporter of the Union) in doing that, and in therefore
being seen to abandon Catholics in Northern Ireland. So I think
that's a very delicate and difficult decision for the Republican state
to make. I think maybe some of the discussions we have had over
this weekend – the constructive discussions – may have shed some
light, or given some indication of how that problem might be
addressed.

James Hawthorne (Chairman, Community Relations Council in Northern Ireland):

This is a partial reply to an earlier question, Chairman. You said, what can we do? I think it's a statistical fact that a larger proportion of the Northern population visits the South than Southerners visit the North – at all levels. It could be down for the match, it could be to visit one of the ports, it could be for tourism reasons. I think that should be looked at. Even at intellectual levels: I was at a conference at Gap of the North – the Brenner pass – run by Co-Operation North not so long ago. And there was a very good piece from a lady about the North. I found out later that she had never even visited us. That didn't diminish what she said, but there are problems of feeling sorry for us in the North, based on the lack of visits and I think greater note should be taken of the efforts we are making to address the problems that we are discussing at this conference, and have been for the last two or three years. And greater credit should be given for things like the Fair Employment legislation. With all its faults, it is a very advanced piece of legislation that is better than the British legislation on race and, as you know, there is no equivalent legislation here in the South. I'm not building a case for the virtues of the North. I'm just saying that our situation would be greatly helped if you came and saw us in action. Much more than you are doing at the moment.

PART IV

WORKSHOP DISCUSSIONS

WORKSHOP DISCUSSIONS

These are the questions which the chairpersons of the workshops and the Conference Chairman used to focus debate and concentrate participants' minds.

Irish Ireland
1. What is the validity and utility of Irishness as a particular culture now? What is the continuing relevance of the Gaelic tradition in language, education, popular and high culture?
2. Is there a new positive sense of Irishness as against the old sense of Irishness, based to varying degrees on anti-Englishness?
3. Is there still an assumption that to be fully Irish you have to be Catholic? Does Irish Ireland mean something different in the North?
4. Which bits of Irish Ireland do we like; which do we not like; which bits do we want to encourage and which to discourage, and how – concretely – can we do that?

British Ireland
1. What today are the nature and extent of the cultural influences coming to the Republic of Ireland from Britain? Are these influences regionally and/or class distinctive?
2. How can these influences be used and adapted in a positive and creative manner? How can they help us to relate to unionists and unionists to us? Should we be looking increasingly for what Ireland has in common with other regions in this archipelago, regions which are distant from London, Brussels, New York and Holywood?
3. What have the Irish in Britain to tell us and can we hear them?
4. Is the notion of Europe a bit of cultural red herring, complicating the cultural influences from Britain a little, but not much?

5. Which bits of British Ireland do we like; which do we not like; which bits do we want to encourage and which to discourage, and how – concretely – can we do that?

Final Conference Session

1. Do Irishness and Britishness matter any more in the Republic of Ireland? How and why do they matter? Are they likely to continue to matter?
2. Does religion matter any more in Ireland's changing consciousness and culture?
3. Are, for example, gender, class and generation more important determinants of culture in Ireland nowadays?

WORKSHOP DISCUSSION I: BRITISH IRELAND

Chairperson: Professor Anthony Clare

Reporter: Dr Eamonn Hughes, Queen's University, Belfast

Introduction

The chairman began by reminding us of the questions we were to address [see previous pages] emphasising some points highlighted in Terence Brown's lecture. He added to the first question about British Ireland: Are the regions of Britain and Ireland equally affected or involved, or differently involved, in the process of Anglicisation?

The discussion concentrated on the first three questions, and four main topics emerged.

The topics

1) British and English influences on, and attitudes to, Ireland and the Irish.
2) The young Irish.
3) The Irish in Britain.
4) The English language and its status in Ireland.

The Discussion

1) *British and English influences on, and attitudes to, Ireland and the Irish*

The first response to the issue of Anglicisation was that while we should not dilute the focus on Britain, it was impossible to speak of Anglicisation without reference to the larger communion of English-speaking countries which constantly modifies our experience of England or Britain. Another delegate remarked that Europe, as well as complicating influences from England, is particularly significant for the next generation of Irish people. Being Irish in Europe is important, not least because other Europeans are interested in Ireland in a way that the English are not.

The next speaker wondered whether there was now anything in Irish culture, North or South, which was not a regional variant of a larger culture. For example, the media and marketing are so strong in popular culture that the minds of younger people are fixed on English football teams, with a few exceptions such as the enthusiasm when Down recently won the All-Ireland.

Attention turned to the media as the main vehicle for carrying cultural influences to the Republic of Ireland. This can be seen even in official attitudes; when RTE2 was being discussed references were made to areas which were deprived because they did not get the three available British channels. The competition between RTE and the Northern television channels for foreign-produced programmes suggests that this is what people want. The World Courts have allocated to Ireland a satellite footprint so that theoretically we could redress the imbalance, but this will probably be sold to international commercial interests and the opportunity will be lost. However, few of the external media influences are actually British; they are Australian and largely American.

Doubts were expressed about this point in that the media are one of the biggest factors in the Anglicisation of Ireland. The Irish language is declining, English influence is becoming stronger, and the worry is that we may become less creative. However, in local radio, in drama and literature there is still a very strong distinctive impulse.

The readership of British newspapers has gone up substantially, especially in Dublin, for a long time. The same is true in the North, which raises a question about the anguish about balance in the media in Northern Ireland. One of the things one notices in England is that we know so much more about them because we watch their media whereas they do not watch Irish media, which is why the retention in Irish hands of the satellite footprint is important.

It was pointed out that the term Anglicisation is misleading. The media do not actually tell us about Britain. They tell us about the south-east of England. This is important in relation to the Unionists whose links traditionally have been with Scotland and with very different kinds of values and traditions. We are not aware of that diversity and that contribution because our phrasing of the question limits our discussion. It was then argued that Anglicisation refers to a specific process by which we are influenced by the culture that is propagated from the South of England with its power, money and media. That, of course, is not the whole of England, let alone Scotland, Wales or Northern Ireland.

The discussion then turned to the aim of education in the North under the Stormont regime which, it was argued, was to produce people who were English rather than British. Given this experience, it might actually be liberating to think in terms of Britishness rather than Englishness. Another speaker then remarked that while the culture promoted through education was English, the political identity was British. Consequently, Northerners while British by passport, can be Irish by addition. This can enrich one's experience, though few share this sense of being enriched and it takes time to arrive at.

Another workshop member said that while we see ourselves disproportionately large, we should also recognise the massive indifference to Ireland in Britain. There is a profound ignorance about Ireland at many levels in Britain. For example, there is only one institution in Britain, which is in a perilous financial condition, seriously engaged in the study of Ireland. Ireland is Britain's major trading partner, and the conflict in the North is the source of its major political and moral crisis. There was agreement that the paucity of serious Irish studies in British academic life was a great academic disgrace. One delegate felt that this may explain why the Irish are often admired for quite the wrong reasons, and accept this because it is a form of attention.

An English seminar member agreed that this situation should be rectified, and added that this should extend beyond the educational sphere. The debate in Britain now is about its multi-racial nature and the Irish do not figure in this debate, because it is doubtful that they constitute an ethnic minority in its terms. There is no creative discussion about the relationship with Northern Ireland. There is also a need for a greater understanding in Britain of the way in which the Republic is developing. The British government and the whole range of cultural, artistic, and educational organisations should be encouraged to take a creative and more constructive interest in the Irish in Britain, and that could lead to attention in Britain being focussed on the relationship with Ireland.

2) *The young Irish*

This part of the discussion focussed on the ways in which young people identify with being Irish. One delegate stated that this identification was both unselfconscious and new. It finds its expression in rock music and a burgeoning Irish theatre which relies on Irish plays. There is a desperate yearning on people's part to see something which talks to them about what it means to be Irish now and in the future. This is quite distinct from the old introspection. The young no longer feel tied to history. Another speaker said that throughout Ireland, including the North, the young are finding ways of expressing themselves, of exploring their history and their identification with an extraordinary confidence. The arts generally seem to be a forum in which Irish people can work towards something new together.

The emphasis we were placing on the experience of young people was challenged on the grounds that the young are much the same everywhere. In this view we were according their activities more significance than was justified; our concentration on them was part of the old problem of treating Ireland as unique. It was explained that in the face of an idea of Irish culture being in retreat it is important that we should be aware of a generation which is interested in these questions but which does not look to the past.

Another delegate wanted to know if we were to regard this as a possible way out of the entrapments of the present; are we going to be conquered by the confidence of the young? The point was made that the young are important because they see no need for the straitjacketed phrasing that we use. They do not define themselves in terms of an official culture North and South which has by and large postulated an Irish-British polarisation. There is a way of living, and an expression of it, that does not require one to be pro-Irish or anti-British. It was then remarked that the young are conscious that they may have to leave Ireland. This is why they think about whether they are going to continue being Irish or whether they will become American or British.

Another delegate pointed out that this long discussion of young people's cultural perceptions had included no one under twenty-five. We need a forum in which articulate young people can express their views of culture and identity. One possible way of having such a forum would be through a media-link between us and the Irish in Britain. This might encourage the British to engage in more study of all aspects of Ireland. It was remarked that this was a rather genteel conference dealing with a very ungenteel subject. The voices that are missing from this conference may be disruptive ones, but we should still try to include such voices so that young people from all classes can interrogate the genteel decision-making generation. The chairman explained that efforts had been made to reach as wide a range as possible for the conference. He acknowledged that different structures are needed to involve as many as possible.

The discussion then turned to the school syllabus in the South. One delegate informed us that there is an Irish Studies 'A' Level in Britain, thanks to the British Association for Irish Studies and the Liverpool Institute of Irish Studies, but there did not seem to be an equivalent Leaving Cert module. There was some confusion as to whether the options available at Leaving Cert are equivalent to the Irish Studies 'A' Level. Discussion then moved to the broader point that the present education systems allow the people of these islands to ignore each other. Education should address itself to the links and relationships between the various traditions. The chairman asked if we were broadly in favour of a recommendation to the Department of Education that a course like the Education for Mutual Understanding course in Northern Ireland should be introduced here. Such a course would consider the relationships between people on this island and within the Irish-British archipelago. There was general agreement to this, with the further suggestion that Education for Mutual Understanding in Northern Ireland should be expanded to include the whole of the archipelago, and not just the two communities.

3) *The Irish in Britain*

In response to an earlier remark, the point was made that the young learn about the Irish in Britain by becoming the Irish in Britain. As such they become literally and metaphorically disenfranchised, because, uniquely in Europe, they are not allowed to vote at home, which contributes to their feeling of being abandoned. The Irish in America are vibrant and confident, and that provides a base for migrants there. The Irish in Britain, on the other hand, are perceived mainly as a problem. Their image, which feeds back into how they feel about themselves, is based partly on a sense of failure, and partly on the problems of the North. This may explain recent research findings that young Irish in Britain are working below their, often high, educational achievements. Their presence in Britain imposes duties on British institutions which should be taken account of at university level, and from there move into the secondary schools. This would improve the position of the Irish in Britain.

It was suggested that the marginalisation of the Irish and ignorance about Ireland was partly the fault of the Irish in Britain. The young gather in Irish communities and do not allow the British to get to know them. Many commute between Britain and Ireland, which has its positive side in maintaining an identity at home. However, alongside the continuing desire to return, the sense of being in exile, that characterises the Irish in Britain, prevents meaningful integration into the culture in which they are living and working. This does not stop them feeling resentful that Ireland has failed them. The young now are going to England for things which are not available here, whether that's abortion, or employment or sundry other things.

We then discussed the confusion in attitudes to emigration. Emigrants do not always fit our stereotypes of them. For example, we think that we know about the Irish in America. However, the majority of the Irish in America are of Protestant descent, deriving from eighteenth-century emigration. We are largely unaware of them partly because we have an image of the Irish in America as Catholic, and partly because they have integrated. Whether it is good or bad that these people have integrated is open to question. There was a challenge to the idea of Protestant integration based on the many groups in Canada and America containing Protestants who identify themselves as Irish. Another speaker reminded us that eighteenth-century Protestant emigrants could integrate more easily than later emigrants because they were in at the founding of the USA. Later emigrants found themselves in an already formed society. This is the experience of Irish emigrants from both religious persuasions in England.

One delegate remarked that, as a returned emigrant, he found that everyone was interested in his views of Ireland, but no one wanted to know about Britain. This suggests that while the British educational establishment must rectify its lamentable failure to study Ireland, there is also a need for more study of the Irish in Britain here as well. Why, for example, have the Irish in Britain no images of achievement to compare with the figure of, say, John F. Kennedy in America? There are, after all, at least two groups of middle-class Irish in Britain; those who regard themselves as fail-

ures and those who are resiliently Irish in Britain. Perhaps we are
not interested in the Irish in Britain because we think that they
have nothing to say to us except that we have failed them, which
merely reinforces their sense of failure and abandonment. The
point about images of achievement was then expanded. Cultural
and ritual significance derives from becoming part of the public
and symbolic domain. Irish Britain has not reached that domain
either in Britain or in Ireland. The absence of the vote is important in both actual and symbolic terms.

The danger of sentimentalising the Irish in Britain was raised.
We have to remember the complete integration and the enormous prosperity of much of the Irish community, and that many
feel freer there than they do here. There are negative aspects no
doubt, but we should also talk about the advantages. While we are
considering alienation we should also address ourselves to the
Northern Protestants who seem to be to us what the Irish in
Britain are to the British: we don't seem to talk to them; they don't
seem to talk to us.

The issue of whether the Irish migrant experience in Britain was
a single-generation phenomenon was discussed. Some felt that the
English seem to assimilate the Irish in one generation, and that
without the constant flow of emigrants the Irish in Britain would
quickly vanish. We over-emphasise the problem and forget that
many Irish over there find England congenial. Others challenged
the idea of assimilation. The emigrant experience can be liberating and enriching but it is also dislocating. It is not just a question
of identifying with another culture, it is also a question of losing a
sense of what one's own culture is. This may be a condition of
twentieth-century life, it may even be healthy, but it is also unset-
tling.

It was then pointed out that to resolve such disagreements
about the Irish in Britain we need much more research. Furthermore, the Irish in Britain are not an homogenous group. This is
what makes the British Association for Irish Studies so necessary.
There is a range of different demands and attitudes to respond to
and a very large area in which little research has been done.

The point about the parallel between the Irish in Britain and
the Northern Protestants was returned to. This analogy, while
loose, is of interest in the context of a discussion about second and
third generation Irish in Britain, and what will become of them,
because of the parallels with Ulster Protestant thinking about the

position of future generations in an altered Ireland. One answer to this is that the Planter experience is of survival of identity. They still describe themselves as British after 400 years. It was pointed out that one reason why they call themselves British after so long is because they were forced into it when the word Ireland was hijacked. Furthermore, young Protestants in the North are leaving. There are still more young Catholics than young Protestants leaving each year, but at the higher levels of educational achievement the balance swings the other way. So many of the young, about whom we have been talking, leaving each year is bound to have a destabilising effect.

4) *The English language and its status in Ireland*
In this part of the discussion we considered the significance of the fact that the theatrical and artistic vitality referred to is in English. There is an awareness that it is not just the language of the neighbouring island. That is an acknowledgement of extraordinary cultural significance in Ireland. We should feel exhilarated by the knowledge that in Ireland authentic indigenous cultural reality can now be expressed in English as well as in Irish, because historically in the South the view was that English expression was somehow inauthentic and to be regretted. To get it into the public record that English is now fully authentic, as the way in which young people express their sense of being Irish on the island and in Britain, is a step forward.

There has been a change since the turn of the century when Irish writers were threatened by the English language. Contemporary Irish writers now feel utterly at home in it, and part of the reason for this is that they are sharing the language with the huge world community which is expressing itself in English. Since English in Ireland is now the language (along with some areas in which Irish still remains a genuine cultural resource) through which we express ourselves, we should safeguard its regionally distinct nature; there is non-standard Irish-English and that's a positive thing. Regional distinctiveness is being reduced by the mass media, particularly through advertising. Certain upmarket products are advertised on RTE using English accents; other products are sold in native accents of one sort or another. We should not simply acquiesce in the face of market research and commercial interests; instead we should insist that advertisers do not insult our ethnicity in this fashion.

There is a need for indigenous English-speaking culture to be officially validated. The two national objectives in the constitution – re-integration of the territory and the restoration of the Irish language – are antithetical demands. You cannot have both while recognising the existence of the people in the North. The problem is to retain Irish as a resource available for all, without excluding people from other traditions in the North and the South. The State should certainly retain the Irish language as an important element in its cultural identikit, but not in an exclusivist way. The Irish language requires official measures of encouragement if it is to flourish in the face of the communication-forces ranged against it. However, the rhetoric and the symbols of the country are out of kilter with the reality. In certain respects there is already a degree of official encouragement for English-language cultural activity through the entertainment industry and the Arts Council. Something could also perhaps be done in the sphere of the constitution. The tone should be of official celebration of both languages. Language should be seen as communication, not as a nationalist symbol.

The language issue is part of a broader question about the need to redefine the limits of our culture to make it more inclusive. It was pointed out that a number of constituencies were missing from this conference: scientists, psychologists etc. Writers are at the moment well represented at these conferences, but they are being asked to go bail for the nation on issues of this sort. It was pointed out that the *Irish Review* is a journal which aims to fulfil this broader cultural agenda.

WORKSHOP DISCUSSION II: BRITISH IRELAND

Chairperson: Professor Edna Longley

Reporter: Ms Eve Patten, Institute of Irish Studies,
Queen's University, Belfast

Summary
The group was invited to discuss the nature of British cultural influences on the Republic of Ireland, and to consider the extent to which such influences were regionally or class distinctive. it emerged from the debate that the 'experience of Britishness' operates on varying levels and through a number of different channels, ranging from the popular media to the teaching of history in schools. The effects of cultural intercourse with Britain were viewed in both positive and negative terms, and seminar contributors were keen to stress the necessity of recognising the complexity of the Republic's relationship with Britain and the North. The discussion gradually shifted, however, to focus on the problems of the Republic of Ireland itself, as a society which, though changing, continues to adhere to monolithic structures and official myths.

Introduction
The Chairperson offered two key-note questions to the group. First, she drew attention to the emergence of psychiatric language in the general conference debate, and in particular the use of the term 'repression'. How far did cultural repression or the repression of diversity permeate the official discourses of the North and the Republic? Secondly, it was suggested that the group might discuss the role of 'cultural particularities' in the relationship between Ireland and Britain. What could be achieved through fostering local cultural interests in common with those of specific regions in 'the other island'?.

Topics Discussed
1. The experience of Britishness in Ireland.
2. History teaching and the transmission of British and Irish culture.
3. Education for Mutual Understanding (EMU).
4. Culture and the problems of the Republic.

1. 'Living in a British world'.

The group sought to define the manner in which British experience was mediated in Ireland. Did the Republic have a problem about admitting to a 'silent Britishness' as a condition of everyday life? The response to this initial question varied, but it was agreed that the British media in the form of popular newspapers and television provide a regular component of Irish cultural consumption. One contributor remarked that the Irish are likely to be extremely well informed about matters such as the British election, and are therefore already living in a version of 'British Ireland'. Another speaker wished to examine the way in which an Irish audience appropriates media output such as English television comedy and makes use of its reference points in ordinary conversation. He argued that domestic Irish culture was 'heavily permeated by Englishness' and that the relationship was largely an unselfconscious one.

While cultural assimilation of this kind was generally accepted, a strong case was made for the emergence of 'a new, positive sense of Irishness' as a result of Ireland's performance in the 1990 World Cup. It was noted that a 'rootless Irish British' generation identified very closely with the Irish football team, despite the dubious nationality of some of its members. An Irish self-consciousness can be seen to exist, therefore, despite constant cultural interaction with Britain. The World Cup experience signified a willingness to reclaim a version of Irishness liberated from many of its complicating preoccupations. There was some disagreement about this, however, and it was also pointed out that in the absence of international or World Cup matches, the Irish tend to support English football-league teams. One speaker regarded this as a form of repression, and evidence of the fact that many people in the Republic consider themselves to exist in a 'mental hinterland'.

The group was also reminded that Britishness itself had various components, including Scottish and Welsh, and that relations with these individual cultures could prove particularly enriching.

It remained important that the Irish had the power of discrimination with regard to the kind of culture in which they chose to share.

2. 'Written out of history'

Following on from this topic, one contributor commented on the workings of British influence in a range of different but less obvious areas; highlighting, as an example, Ireland's adoption of English methods and theory in the development of the conservation and local history movements. These had provided the means for a fresh appreciation of the past, and local history in particular offered a means of contact with Scotland and Wales, providing scope for 'a four nation encounter' around local communities.

This brought reaction on the subject of history in general. One participant observed that previous Unionist parliamentary representation in Dun Laoghaire in 1918 did not feature in historical accounts of the period, and that this was a typical instance of how an undesirable presence was simply written out of history. In turn, complaints were voiced about an education system in the North which had suppressed Irish history, and a contributor noted that Northern historical knowledge of the Republic was surprisingly limited as a result.

Historians and teachers in the group were then asked if the situation of history teaching in this respect had changed in recent years. It was suggested that the curriculum had improved as a result both of increased liaison between schools and academics, and the production of better textbooks. The 'affirmative' or ideological use of history by certain bodies had not been eroded completely, but new attempts to locate Irish history positively within European history in general had proved successful. Some contributors were quick to point out that problems in the teaching of history were not limited to the Northern Irish educational system, and one speaker described how in schools in the Republic, sensitive subjects such as the Reformation or Cromwell were frequently given simplistic and one-sided treatment.

3. EMU 'The tip of the ice-berg'

This area of discussion prompted enquiries concerning the progress and achievements of the Education for Mutual Understanding programme. Speaking on behalf of the project, one contributor stated that it had affected only the tip of the iceberg, and that a great deal of work remained to be done. EMU was still at a developing stage, exploring various possibilities. However, it was recognised that the preparation of new core-curriculum material in the subjects of religion and history marked significant progress. With the increase in the number of integrated schools in the North, Catholic authorities in education were being forced to promote EMU, and its representatives noted an increased readiness to trust the movement on the part of both communities. Even situations of vehement opposition from parents were seen to be useful in that they forced arguments and prejudices into the open, creating a healthier atmosphere for debate.

There was a warm response from the seminar participants to this report on EMU's efforts. One speaker noted that the education system in the South was also at fault in perpetuating a Catholic ethos across a range of subjects, and suggested that the Republic needed a similar education programme. Various cross-community ventures and educational initiatives were hindered, however, by lack of provision for teacher-training. It was mentioned that the Cultural Heritage project had run into similar difficulties: teachers interested in the movement and its material were given insufficient time and facilities to attend conference sessions or receive in-service training.

4. Culture in the Republic: 'Public responsibility and private action'.

A contributor queried the significance of the term 'cultural diversity' in the monocultural society of the Republic, in contrast to its meaning in a society such as Canada. Drawing upon his experience of the Canadian system he highlighted the danger of turning the notion of cultural diversity into a 'cultural pacification' programme, and ultimately damaging a society. Others were supportive of cultural diversity as a reality in the Republic: Irish people were seen to be interested in celebrating their heritage and in exploring their origins. It was accepted, however, that the ethnic composition of Ireland was very different from that of Canada, and this gave rise to a suggestion that Ireland perhaps exports its diversity. Another speaker pointed out that the dangers of difference tend to provoke fear and denial within a society. It emerged from the debate that cultural diversity remains open to various differing interpretations, but many participants agreed with the speaker's suggestion that the concept will work only if it extends beyond the culture of two or three communities, and takes into account other historical strands such as feminism.

The group went on to discuss the nature of culture itself: who shapes culture within a society, and how can we ensure that those living on the margins of the community are involved in the process? New possibilities must be created across a wider spectrum, and this will require radical changes in present social structure and discourse. One speaker also raised the question of a class-division between low and high culture, and highlighted the problem of resistance either to high or low culture from some sectors of the community. Culture identified as 'leisured', 'imperial' or 'alien' was often rejected by those unwilling to risk accusations of 'ethnic betrayal', while popular culture was frequently ignored by funding bodies and organisations. The resultant stasis represented a denial of cultural expression, and must be replaced by a new cultural mobility in Irish society.

As the discussion moved towards a close, it became clear that problems rooted in the cultural and social systems of the Republic remained stumbling blocks. Several contributors attempted to define the negative effects of a pervasive Catholic ethos on various aspects of life, including art and education. It was suggested that a new solidarity ought to challenge this power, but some participants argued that the divorce and abortion referenda had already shown such attempts to be futile. This gave rise to a major dispute in the group. Some were confident that the monolithic structure of the Republic was disintegrating; others remained adamant that an 'institutional diktat' would continue to be forced on a 'secular society'.

While no single conclusion was possible at this juncture, it was generally agreed that leadership in the Republic needs to adopt a radical profile, and that influential individuals must be seen to take decisive action. For its own sake, before it even began to consider its relationship with the North, the Republic must examine the hypocritical basis of its society. In the words of one contributor, it must seek to close the division between 'public responsibility and private action'.

WORKSHOP DISCUSSION III: IRISH IRELAND

Chairperson: Mr Justice Niall McCarthy

Reporter: Dr Chris Morash, St. Patrick's College, Maynooth

'Language . . . exists only in virtue of a kind of contract agreed between
the members of a community'.
                                                            Ferdinand de Saussure

Had a casual observer walked into the room during the deliberations of Workshop III, it is highly unlikely that she or he would
have guessed that the group had been asked to discuss the concept of 'Irish-Ireland'. The phrase 'Irish-Ireland' simply did not
enter into the debate. We should not, I think, dismiss this devia-
tion from the proposed agenda as mere accident. Instead, we
should understand it as the function of a growing awareness that
if the Irish cultural debate is to move forward, a new vocabulary
must be found. More precisely, by ignoring the term 'Irish-
Ireland' as an object of analysis, the group's discussions can be
read as a rejection of the binary opposition – 'Irish-Ireland/
English-Ireland' – which is so often presented as the natural form
for discussing 'the cultures of Ireland'. In ignoring this binary
opposition, the group implicitly asserted the constrictive nature of
all such binary oppositions, and the need to free ourselves of
them.

The opening contribution to the debate set the tone for much
that was to follow by reminding us that whenever we discuss
'culture' that we do so from, and on behalf of, a particular culture.
'Whatever baggage one carries', argued one contributor, 'needs
to be declared before beginning any confrontation or debate'. A
number of participants developed this self-interrogative theme,
pointing out the need to remind ourselves that most of the participants in the present conference were middle-class and middle-

aged; and that any discussion which was to take account of the totality of relationships linking the 'cultures of Ireland' must hear from other social groups. There is an urgent need, one speaker argued, for the 'harsh and horrible reality of life for many, both in the North and in the Republic, to be translated from the language of academic debate'. By phrasing our discussion purely in the language of the liberal humanism of a small, relatively cohesive group, it was suggested, we were excluding the voices of many on the island.

This last observation led to the suggestion that in considering the minority discourses of present-day Ireland, we find a way of re-imagining our past. Wolfe Tone's assertion that Irish freedom will arise from 'that numerous and respectable class of the community, the men of no property' was, for much of the nineteenth century, claimed as the slogan of an exclusivist romantic nationalism. John Mitchel's militant newspaper of the 1848, *The United Irishman*, for instance, printed it as a banner over Mitchel's impassioned editorials. We can, however, reclaim Tone's words from the context into which they were placed by Mitchel, if we interpret them to mean that we can only enter into a 'free' debate by recognising that an increasing percentage of the population – the 'men [and women] of no property' – are excluded from existing cultural paradigms; and that this 'numerous and respectable class' must partake of future cultural formations.

The process of freeing present debates from past interpretations was emphasised by a second speaker, who argued that history – and hence concepts of 'Irishness' and Irish culture – are not ontologically stable entities, but are undergoing constant revision. Indeed, the tendency to frame discussions of Irish culture in terms of an exclusive 'either/or' opposition can be understood as the product of an outmoded way of understanding the Irish past. A.J.P. Taylor's assertion that 'there is no townland in Ireland where blood has not been spilt' was taken as an example of this way of thinking, insofar as it ignores the fact that there is virtually no 'townland' in Europe which could not make a similar claim. If a blood-soaked soil were a cause of social failure, it was argued, Paris (the site of a succession of revolutions and invasions) should today be a cultural and social wasteland – and such was patently not the case. We should not, therefore, feel ourselves inhibited by the past, for the past is simply the product of interpretation, and as such is a product of the present.

A debate concerning the nature of colonisation emerged from this discussion of history, giving a focus to the proposition of an inherently unstable past. Irish culture, one speaker urged, was shaped by two forms of colonialism – English and Catholic. In continuing to see the Irish situation as part of an Anglo-Irish colonial matrix, one runs the risk of ignoring the dominant colonial influence in Ireland today. Another speaker indicated an awareness of this form of colonialism in the emphasis which is so often placed upon the word '*Roman*' when the Roman Catholic church is discussed in a Northern context. Taking up this revised concept of colonial identity, it was suggested by one delegate that English imperial aspirations have all but disappeared. We can measure the degree to which this abatement has taken place, he argued, by reminding ourselves that the late Ian Gow's Westminster seat was taken by Labour, in spite of the best efforts of the Conservative candidate to make Gow's assassination by the IRA an election issue.

With the introduction of the words 'colonial' and 'Catholic' into the debate, it was objected that the very use of such words introduced a falsifying simplicity to the group's deliberations. A number of participants urged the dismantling of monolithic definitions of Catholicism and Protestantism. This is a point which has been made many times in the past in relation to the use of the word 'Protestant' to cover groups as diverse as Methodists, Anglicans, Presbyterians, Baptists, and Free Presbyterians. One thinks, for instance, of Terence Brown's 1985 Field Day pamphlet, *The Whole Protestant Community: The Making of a Historical Myth*. The situation of being referred to as a 'non-Catholic', claimed one Anglican contributor, suggested an 'appalling prospect' of the degree to which the diversity of the Protestant tradition has been misunderstood in Ireland, and in the Republic in particular.

Moreover, the same awareness of cultural diversity needs to be made in relation to the Catholic tradition. 'There is no monolithic Catholic church anymore,' claimed a lay Catholic theologian; 'there is a revolutionary movement within the Catholic church'. In spite of its hierarchical organisational structure, Catholicism is capable of supporting a diversity of theological opinions. This last observation led to a discussion of the radical potential of a recent strain of Catholic thought centring around the area of liberation theology.

Speaking as an Ulster Evangelical Presbyterian, another delegate found this Catholic radicalism a heartening prospect. Many forms of Evangelical Protestantism, he argued, were deeply imbued with the radicalism which provided the fundamental basis for liberal democracy. This was supported by a Southern Baptist speaker, who foresaw the emergence of a new model of nonconformist radical dissent. If it were possible for the radical elements in the Evangelical faiths to come together with their counterparts in the Catholic tradition, he argued, it might be possible to forge a new set of theological alliances which transcended the post-Reformation Catholic/Protestant polarity.

The possibility of such a reconciliation led the next speaker to issue a plea to Catholic laity to show Evangelical Protestants of all creeds that spirituality – and not social or political programmes – were at the heart of their beliefs. On that basis, he claimed, it would be possible to find a common ground which might lead to a union of the radical elements in all traditions. Echoing these words, another speaker argued that although the increasing secularisation of Irish society is often seen as the force which will eradicate the old sectarian antagonisms, it might equally prove to be the force which undermines the spirituality which could heal the wounds of the past. Indeed, for many of the delegates in the group, the assumption of a common spirituality provided a hopeful prospect. Few attempted, however, to define what they meant by the term 'spirituality', and the reliance placed upon such a vague term with subjective referents might point to a future impasse in the development of cultural debate in a theological context.

Anticipating this impasse in one of the most incisive contributions of the morning, one speaker identified the centrality of language to any debate. 'Language', wrote the Swiss linguist, Ferdinand de Saussure early in this century, 'exists only in virtue of a kind of contract agreed between the members of a community'. The workshop was reminded that in a community in which there are a number of mutually exclusive social contracts in operation, language itself becomes a problematic issue. For instance, the use of the word 'Gospel' by Non-conformists in the Irish Republic would differ from the use of the word by their co-regionalists in the North. The speaker went on to query the use of the definite article when the Catholic church is referred to as '*The* Church'. Other words identified as central to any discussion of the cultures of Ireland were 'Fenian' (as an historical term and as a term of abuse) and 'Evangelical' in all of its many social and theological alignments.

In identifying the problematic nature of syntax and vocabulary in the Irish cultural debate, the group identified an area requiring major work. Several speakers from the North expressed their surprise at the personal, anecdotal nature of so many of the contributions to the conference. The 'self-revelatory nature' of the previous night's debate, noted one speaker, 'would not be found in the North'. While many of the more anecdotal contributions were moving, entertaining or illuminating, they are indicative of a state of theoretical impasse. If one can only speak in terms of immediate personal experience, and if that experience is shaped by the damaging binary oppositions of the past (Irish/English; Catholic/Protestant; Nationalist/Unionist) the prospect of transcending those oppositions is curtailed. This is not to say that recognition of the subjective, social nature of any utterance was not seen by the workshop delegates as an encouraging prospect; it was. However, it also served to highlight the limitations of such forms of debate in the absence of a shared theoretical framework which goes beyond personal, anecdotal experience arising from similar class and generational backgrounds. Indeed, it may be that until such as metalanguage is found, the old binary oppositions will continue to be recycled until they become irrelevant to a generation with other experiences and other aspirations. 'Irish Ireland? What does "Irish-Ireland" mean?' asked one participant. 'It may be that we are writing a textbook here for a generation who no longer care about the oppositional terms over which we are battling'.

WORKSHOP DISCUSSION IV: IRISH IRELAND

Chairperson: Dr Margaret MacCurtain

Reporter: Mr Richard Haslam, St Patrick's College, Maynooth

Introduction
The members of the workshop introduced themselves and the session began with a proposal that, in order to maximise the amount of discussion and participation, the group should at some stage organise into sub-groups, each of which would eventually report back to the main group. The proposal was adopted and it was decided that, after an initial group discussion of Question 1 on the worksheets, the sub-groups would discuss Questions 2–3. After the sub-groups had delivered their reports, there would follow a concluding plenary discussion, during which various recommendations could be outlined.

Topics for Discussion
1. What is the validity and utility of Irishness as a particular culture now? What is the continuing relevance of the Gaelic tradition in language, education, popular and high culture?
2. Is there a new positive sense of Irishness as against the old sense of Irishness, based to varying degrees on anti-Englishness?
3. Is there still an assumption that to be fully Irish you have to be Catholic? Does Irish Ireland mean something in the North?
4. Which bits of Irish-Ireland do we like; which do we not like; which bits do we want to encourage and which to discourage, and how – concretely – can we do that?

Group Discussion of Question 1
Referring to the paper on 'Irish Ireland' given that morning by Gearóid O'Tuathaigh, and that on 'British Ireland' given by Terence

Brown, one participant in the workshop argued that the stated goal of a non-exclusive Irish language, culture, and identity was as fraught with difficulty as the achievement of a northern Protestant culture which would be prepared fully to acknowledge and incorporate its Irish dimension. It was further claimed that many northern nationalists felt themselves cut off from the South, and that they approved of the Anglo-Irish Agreement less for any intrinsic merit it possessed than for its ability to annoy northern unionists.

This contribution identified a theme reiterated in many of the contributions that ensued: namely, that the question of division or diversity in the cultures of Ireland could not be phrased coherently until it was recognised that northern nationalists, southern nationalists, northern Catholics and southern Catholics did not share exactly the same cultural assumptions; neither did northern unionists, southern unionists, northern Protestants or southern Protestants. Rather than consisting of a series of uncomplicated North-South, and Protestant-Catholic binary oppositions, the political, religious and social cultures of Ireland had long since proliferated into a multiplicity of intersecting or non-intersecting formations.

A group member from Northern Ireland observed that the distinctiveness of the north-eastern part of the island dated back many centuries and had been noted, for example, by Wesley when passing through Newry in 1750 (many other recognitions of radical difference were included in Roy Foster's recent history of modern Ireland). It was claimed that the distinctive Protestant 'ethos' included an anti-authoritarian refusal to accept imposed control. The 'legal fiction' of Articles 2 and 3 of the Republic's constitution, however, maintained incorrectly that no difference between the two parts of Ireland existed; because of this basic inaccuracy, Articles 2 and 3 deserved to be altered in and of themselves, and not as part of a barter with unionists. A final claim from this contributor was that the Anglo-Irish Agreement, like Articles 2 and 3, also signally ignored or played down those cultural distinctions between North and South which refuted the argument for homogenisation.

The attention of the group was then directed to the cross-curricular educational programmes of 'Cultural Heritage' and 'Education for Mutual Understanding' which had been introduced into Northern Irish schools: it was suggested that a similar programme in Republic of Ireland schools would alert pupils to the specificities of northern unionist, nationalist, Protestant and Catholic cultural traditions, as well as leading them to consider diversity in their own societies. Some progress in North-South understanding was already being achieved at a post-school level, under the auspices of Co-Operation North, which had facilitated 'twinning' arrangements between a large number of Women's Groups on either side of the Border.

At this stage in the discussion, the group divided into five sub-groups in order to address Questions 2–4. After twenty minutes, these sub-groups reported back on their findings.

Report of Sub-Group 1
Young people were seen as a focus for radical change throughout Ireland, since they were beginning to re-read history and discover identities beyond previously narrow religious constraints. In order to facilitate this process, it was vital that the Churches guided change rather than promoted polarisation. Exchange programmes, such as those encouraged by Co-Operation North, indicated a very positive direction to follow. However difficult it might be, a climate of optimism had to be fostered, not just to raise the morale of despondent communities, but also because it was an indispensable and urgent factor in the creation of economic growth: healing processes between the various traditions were much more likely to succeed in an environment where opportunities for employment and renewed self-esteem were once more available.

Report of Sub-Group 2
It was felt necessary to identify and encourage existing 'successes', where people of different cultural traditions could relate without problems: obvious examples could be seen in the area of sport, such as the rugby and soccer World Cups. However, the underlying tensions often manifested in symbols of group identity could perhaps be recognised in the lack of interest or sense of exclusion experienced by certain sections of the northern population with respect to Down's recent G.A.A. All-Ireland victory. In conclusion, it was maintained that the political task in Europe over the next century was to discover new procedures which could allow differing ethnic and religious groups to participate fully in social and political life, without coming into conflict or repeating the formulas of the past; some political formation more flexible than the unitary nation-state had to be developed.

Report of Sub-Group 3

Significant differences between northern and southern Catholics were believed to exist. It was claimed that, while Europe could not be used as an excuse to bury the differences between the northern communities, the European Community could, through a net-work of regional contacts, establish working forums to discuss and re-define national identity throughout the rapidly changing western and eastern European countries: during such a process, new and possibly fruitful perspectives on specifically Irish manifestations of ethnic and religious strife could be produced. On a smaller scale, university contacts and grant distribution arrangements between Great Britain, Northern Ireland and the Republic needed to be re-assessed and developed.

Report of Sub-Group 4

An attempt was made to explain the acknowledged differences between northern and southern Catholics: it was argued that nationalism usually defines itself first by means of opposition and, since there was plenty of opposition in the North, northern nationalists still adhered to a pre-1920 form of nationalism. However, with the achievement of independence in the South, the traditional forms of opposition dissolved and no simple focus for national identity remained, with the result that the old ideology was falling apart. What was important was to replace simple oppositional notions of national identity with complex ones. Although the main rationale for the language movement was that it provided a possible anchor for identity, it was not clear if the official language or majority religion of one part of Ireland was sufficiently 'complex' to generate widely inclusive notions of identity.

Report from Sub-Group 5

Taking up a concept from Gearóid O'Tuathaigh's paper, members of this sub-group queried how it was possible to achieve 'particularity without exclusivity'? If the possibility of a 'restoration' of earlier cultural formations was ruled out, but the necessity of 'continuity' was advocated, the question then raised was: is continuity possible? Perhaps continuity of a narrow and exclusive sort was possible in the North, but it did not seem to be a viable option any longer in the South. The only hope for restoring continuity as a positive and vital force lay in addressing and working through discontinuity and alienation in the most urgent way. Perhaps what we required in order to highlight our cultural particularities was to find someone elsewhere in Europe who would tell us how important an issue it was – then we could 'steal' the idea.

Concluding Discussion

One member of the workshop expressed surprise that little attention had been paid to the influence of the modern media on 'Irishness': young people throughout the South now had access to a multi-channel culture. In reply, it was suggested that the diversity of television programming was certain to undermine received ideas of Irishness, but it was unclear whether this diversity was likely to replace the older concepts with something more or less useful.

In order to counteract the third-level 'brain-drain' in the North, as a result of which many northern Protestants are going to British rather than northern or southern universities, it was felt that some form of co-ordination between the university systems of Northern Ireland and the Republic should be established in order to encourage more northern Protestants and Catholics to come to the South, and (just as importantly) to encourage southern Catholics and Protestants to attend university in the North.

Another participant in the workshop noted that 'youth' had been identified as an issue of major importance, but she maintained that it was important to introduce further differentiations within this rather unitary concept. Those who have access to higher education are generally less aware of oppression and harrassment than those who have limited or no access: in other words, the issue of ethnicity should not be allowed to cloak that of wealth and class. Any proposals for increasing awareness of cultural particularities which did not also address radical economic disparities concerning access to education and exposure to violence were non-starters.

The chairperson concluded the discussion with the observation that (as Seamus Deane has argued) our history is one of discontinuities: both in the North and in the South, discontinuity is the dynamic of our cultural lives.

RECOMMENDATIONS

1. 'Cultural Heritage' and 'Education for Mutual Understanding' cross-curricular programmes should be introduced into schools in the Republic of Ireland.

2. Further exchange and twinning groups, similar to those organised by Co-Operation North and various women's groups on both sides of the Border, should be actively encouraged.

3. Greater liaison between northern and southern universities should be established, in order to encourage students from the South to go North to study and vice versa (financial incentives would make such exchanges a more attractive proposition).

4. European Community programmes to discuss both growing ethnic diversity and new and more flexible concepts of national identity should be instituted.

PART V

RELIGIOUS IRELAND

CHAIRMAN'S INTRODUCTION

Ladies and gentlemen, we now come to the part of our agenda, described in the conference programme as 'Religious Ireland'. This section was to have been chaired by Simon Lee, the Professor of Jurisprudence at Queen's University, Belfast. Unfortunately he has been unable to return today and sends his apologies. I feel particularly ill-equipped to chair a debate on religious Ireland, and recognise that I have none of Professor Lee's qualifications for this task.

The first speaker will be Thomas Kilroy, who is a novelist and playwright as you all know. He will speak from the point of view of a secularised person in contemporary society.

The second speaker in this section of the programme will be David Stevens, the Associate Secretary of the Irish Council of Churches. David will argue for the centrality of religion in Irish culture and look at the position of Protestants in the Republic.

Finally, Sister Helena O'Donoghue, President of the Conference of Major Religious Superiors, will distinguish between religion as an identity card and as faith, and will argue for a holistic culture with religion as an integral part of it.

Religious Ireland (I)

THOMAS KILROY

Secularised Ireland

There is a lot of fear in Ireland. Yesterday, Brendan Kennelly talked about the fear of women but I don't think this is confined to Ireland. It will remain pervasive while the unfinished business of admitting women into full, unambiguous freedom in the world, continues.

I am thinking, rather, of a kind of modality of fear at the root of Irish culture, a kind of timidity before life itself in all its mortal glory and all its dreadful horror, its inexpressible variety. People who are afraid of life will always try to restrict the lives of others. We have many examples of restrictiveness in contemporary Ireland and many examples of individuals and institutions which seek to control and restrict the actions of others. We even have the ultimate restriction at the point of a gun.

I have to say that I believe that the peculiar nature of the fear I'm talking about has its source in education, particularly that directed by the two most politically assertive churches on this island, the Roman Catholic and Presbyterian: education in the widest sense, in the classroom, from the pulpit but also in politics.

I want to address the subject of fear for a few minutes and I would ask you to interpret everything I say politically, since I won't have time to make all the connections myself. I want to talk about the way fear generates violence. I want to talk about the way it perverts and distorts moral values: the way it produces a pathological politics, forms of tyranny, even if the ostensible political mode is a democratic one.

One of the principal sources of fear, in the individual as in the community, is a sense of severe disconnectedness, a deep insecurity where the familiar stepping-stones disappear from beneath our feet.

A void opens up between what we have been and what we might become. For this reason, fear is a paralysing of the possibility of development and is frequently most acute when the possibility of development is greatest.

A positive outcome of fear leads to transformation, a leap across the void since fear is a signal to us that we must change or calcify. Fear is an invitation to becoming although it manifests itself as rigidity, in an urge to retreat or escape.

A negative outcome of fear, on the other hand, solidifies this helplessness and hopelessness. The very failure to move, to change, to risk creates, firstly, a highly exaggerated sense of the value of what we are and what we hold. This is a spurious consolation for being unable to become something else or to acquire a different set of possessions. This, in turn, passes to a secondary negative phase in which the fear-ridden mind tries to project its dilemma, its failure, on to another or others since the first condition, that of false self-importance, quickly becomes intolerable under stress. It is at this point that fear generates violence, a destructiveness of the self, of another or others that can be both psychic and physical.

I'm trying to describe a condition of character that is immediately recognisable to a writer or, indeed, a reader of imaginative literature. The literary example that I think of now is the great first act of Shakespeare's *Macbeth* in which a man of fine sensibility is seduced into murder by a woman, his wife, who relentlessly plays upon his fear of effeminacy. The individual gripped by fear is extremely vulnerable and open to manipulation, particularly to a playing upon character weakness. The community gripped by fear is similarly vulnerable and equally open to manipulation by simplistic politics which plays upon its insecurities.

You may well ask what all this has to do with our discussions? What bearing does the psychology of fear have upon the values, moral and political, by which we live in the Republic? It is relatively easy, I think, to see its bearing upon the appalling situation in the North. It is certainly easy to see fear as one of the blockages to any creative discourse between North and South.

One reason why I'm taking this oblique approach is that I believe attention to structural changes, rearrangements, meetings, communications and the like are no longer enough. The central question on this island is not so much division as the sub-rational nature of the divisiveness, the fact that despite the library of books on the subject it will not yield itself to rational analysis, the fact that despite the great efforts of politicians of good-will it is resistant, and will continue to be resistant, to political initiatives, the fact that the fierce power of this divisiveness is subliminal, hidden, which makes it extremely difficult to confront – but confront it we must.

We in the South are afraid of the North. We are understandably afraid of its violence. We are afraid of being saddled with its costly security bill. But we are also afraid of its passion, its uncompromising feeling, its hard directness of expression. We are afraid of its religious mix and particularly of coming into any closer contact with its Protestant communities. All of these things shake established orders of power and styles of living in the South. They threaten not only the old nationalism but also, and more importantly, the new and rather gauche cosmopolitanism of the Republic, the self-consciously styled 'European' Ireland with its own place at the Euro-table, its new money, new scandals, new insecurities. On those occasions when we present ourselves in our new finery before the world we are fearful of the North, as one would be of an unpredictable relative in the attic.

In the North, on the other hand, the mutual fear is so profound that it has allowed each side to demonise the other. This is a truism. At this stage I had better declare myself. I believe that what we have in this conflict is a classic confrontation between two sects, sustained by territorial claims and a history of bloodshed, comparable, that is, to the enmity between Arab and Jew, Hindu and Muslim, Croat and Serb, about which the late Hubert Butler wrote so eloquently. What gives all these conflicts their dark potency is the claim of the Elect, the Chosen People, the One, True Faith, in other words the claim of unique access to divine truth. This claim on one side is intolerable to the other since if it were true it would immediately undermine the other faith. One cannot exaggerate the rage and terror which such absolutism inspires, nor the barbarity which it is capable of causing.

Outside this country this is how our predicament is understood. It is further understood as one of those pre-modern relics, like nationalism, left-overs which history has failed to exorcise and which is distinctly at odds with any civilised idea of progress. The upsurge of religious fanaticism and extreme nationalism today is seen, from this point of view, as a late reaction to the inevitable globalisation of human culture and the increase of secularisation. What is particularly terrifying about these religious conflicts is that even when the individual cause, Arab, Jew or Christian, becomes secularised some cloak of righteousness persists, the cause retains this sense of absolute justification, even when the political reality states otherwise.

In Ireland the Christian churches have been distancing themselves from the mess. They rightly condemn the atrocities and rightly point out that anyone involved cannot claim membership of a church which teaches love and forgiveness. But they are also saying that this conflict has nothing to do with religion. I find this incomprehensible and a dreadful evasion of responsibility. Without wishing to be offensive, I think the Christian churches should be down on their collective knees begging the forgiveness of the Irish people for the horrors visited upon this island in the name of Christianity. More temperately, I would hope that the churches would begin a process of self-searching into those all too human, all too fallible elements in their structures, such as education, which help to foment intolerance and lethal ignorance.

In 1987 Seamus Deane contributed a paper to a symposium on reconciliation sponsored by the Irish School of Ecumenics. Here is how his paper concludes:

> A culture is not an entity which can safely or enduringly base itself upon the grounds of race or religion or territory. These are childish and dangerous concepts. They did have force, no doubt, at one time; but it is so long ago that it has almost passed out of mind. Unfortunately, since the nineteenth century, these concepts gained a new force and currency; in modern conditions, their effects were explosive. A mature culture is based on a political idea, not on racial essence, religious faith, or nostalgia for an historic territory. What Ireland needs is such a political concept. Neither that of the Republic nor that of the United Kingdom suffices any longer, because each is, by now, sectarianised. The Christian religions play themselves false if they assume their fate is bound up with the preservation of either. In doing so, they are mistaking the message of the Book of Revelation and misconstruing a political for a spiritual apocalypse. Religious literalism breeds political fanaticism and prevents emergence of either a true conception of religion or the possibility of a true political idea. It would help the present situation if the distinction (not necessarily the separation) between Church and

State were acknowledged by the Churches. Once admitted, then the Churches could again become part of our culture, rather than the translators of culture into literal and lethal politics.[1]

A political idea for the future freed of territorial claims, freed of religious claims, freed of racial distinctiveness. It seems pretty hopeless, doesn't it? And yet if this year has taught us anything, it is that incredible acceleration of political change can take place once people can move beyond their fears. Such an idea will only emerge here when a sufficient swell of opinion comes into existence which will by-pass the extremists, both the militarists and the politicians, on either side and release the populations that presently support them. As a political idea it can only have the simplest of goals, a dedication to the sharing of this island in peace. As a moral idea it will have to be completely secularised.

Let me explain how I use this word secularised. Many of you will be familiar with Harvey Cox's book *The Secular City* which created something of a sensation when it first appeared in the States in the sixties. Cox is now the Victor Thomas Professor of Religion at Harvard but was a young Protestant theologian when he first wrote the book as a source text for a particular conference of American Young Christians. The book simply took off, clearly articulating something which needed to be said, and its influence has been diverse, on Liberation Theology in South America, for instance, and on much American thinking about the problematic conditions of the modern city.

The central idea of *The Secular City* is an acceptance that we are rapidly moving into a secularised, highly urbanised phase of human history with the rapid disappearance of tribal, traditional values. The relevance of all of this to contemporary Ireland is obvious. The two striking images which Cox has thought up for this technopolitan new age are: The Man on the Giant Switchboard, man, that is, at the hub of a gigantic information system and The Man in the Cloverleaf, that is, at the centre of one of those intricate intersections so characteristic of American highways. Communication, then, and mobility and both on a scale undreamt of in the past.

This world, according to Cox, is by its very nature secularised. Far from resisting it as a theologian he embraces it, and his book is a search for God, for a new theology, on the streets of the secular city:

The thesis of *The Secular City* was that God is just as present in the
secular as in the religious realms of life, and we unduly cramp
the divine presence by confining it to some specially delineated
spiritual or ecclesial realm. This idea has two implications. First,
it suggests that people of faith need not flee from the allegedly
godless contemporary world. But second, it also means that not
all religion is good for the human spirit. The thesis was certainly
not original with me. Indeed, the presence of the holy within
the profane is suggested by the doctrine of the Incarnation, not
a recent innovation. As for a suspicion of religion, both Jesus
and the Hebrew prophets lashed out at some of the religion
they saw around them. God *in* the secular: not an original idea
but one that needs to be restated time and again. And today is
surely no exception.[2]

Last year, for a reissue of the book in the States, Cox wrote a new
introduction. In it he had to respond to the recent upsurge of
religious fundamentalism and the reappearance of militant, tribal
nationalism in many parts of the globe which would seem to
undermine his thesis. Quite the contrary, is his response:

> If anything, I believe these developments make the central
> thesis of *The Secular City* even more credible. I argued then that
> secularisation – if it is not permitted to calcify into an ideology
> (which I called 'sectarian') – is not everywhere and always an
> evil. It frees religious groups from their own theocratic preten-
> sions and allows people to choose among a wider range of
> ethical and spiritual options. Today, in parallel fashion, it seems
> obvious that the resurgence or religion in the world is not
> everywhere and always a *good* thing. Do the long-suffering peo-
> ple of Iran believe that after the removal of their ruthless shah,
> the installation of a quasi-theocratic Islamic republic has turned
> out to be a wholly positive move? Do those Israelis and Palestin-
> ians who yearn for a peaceful settlement of the West Bank
> bloodletting believe that either the Jewish or the Moslem reli-
> gious parties are helping? The truth is that both the religious
> revival and secularisation are morally ambiguous processes. We
> still desperately need what I tried to sketch out in 1965, a way of
> welcoming a pluralism of worldviews that does not deteriorate
> into nihilism and a sober recognition that both religious and
> secular movements are morally ambiguous. Both can become

either the bearers of emancipation or the avatars of misery, or some of each. Wouldn't a modest sprinkling of secularisation, a dereligionising of the issues come as a welcome relief in Ulster, and help resolve the murderous tensions in Kashmir and the Gaza Strip?[3]

This is an extremely readable book written with a cheery American pragmatism but one should not underestimate its profundity. It speaks of a faith that is far removed from the sad, withered sense of religion so often experienced on this island, North and South and I only wish it could be widely read here.

References

1. Seamus Deane, 'Reconciliation of Cultures: Apocalypse Now!' in *Reconciling Memories*, ed. Alan D. Falconer (The Columba Press: Dublin, 1988), pp 28–29.
2. Harvey Cox, *The Secular City* (Collier Books: New York, 1990), p xii.
3. Cox, ibid, pp xi–xii.

Religious Ireland (II)

DAVID STEVENS

Protestants in the Republic

In Seamus Heaney's latest collection *Seeing Things* there is a poem
entitled 'The Settle Bed' and I would like to begin by reading you
a few lines:

Yet I hear an old sombre tide awash in the headboard:
Unpathetic *och ochs* and *och hohs*, the long bedtime
Anthems of Ulster, unwilling, unbeaten,

Protestant, Catholic, the Bible, the beads . . .

I come before you as a representative of the 'old sombre tide'. I
want to come back to Heaney's poem in a moment, but one of the
interesting things about the cultural traditions debate in the North
of Ireland has been the absence of discussion about the 'old
sombre tide'; or maybe it is thought that the tide has finally gone
out. Anyway, religion appears to be the great unmentionable. I
want to insist, in the words of Heaney in the poem I have already
quoted, that it is the 'un-get-roundable weight'.

Churches are the oldest continuous institutions in this society.
The religious assemblies of the Irish, Scots and English carry the
memories of community experience, North and South. They are
entwined with, cannot be separated from, the cultural and political histories of the different communities in Ireland. They have
shaped every-one in this society, believers and non-believers. They
affect how we carry on our politics. They continue to be the focal
point of much of community and personal relationships as Duncan
Morrow has shown for Northern Ireland in his recent report *The
Churches and Inter-Community Relationships*.[1] Churches carry through

their ritual, organisation and activity much of the received culture of the community. They are the most important institutions through which a sense of a whole island belonging together is maintained. Their gathered assemblies are one of the few places where Northerner and Southerner meet together.

Religion is that which binds together. It has also brought diversity and division in Ireland. It is that interaction between binding together, diversity and division which is central to the Irish problem, and central to the cultural traditions debate.

Attempts to ignore or evade the reality of the centrality of religion in the experience of Irish people, both North and South, will fundamentally skew and invalidate the debate. It is here I wish to return to Heaney's poem 'The Settle Bed'. After talking of the 'un-get-roundable weight' he goes on

. . . But to conquer that weight,

Imagine a dower of settle beds tumbled from heaven,
And some nonsensical vengeance come on the people,
Then learn from that harmless barrage that whatever is given

Can always be reimagined . . .

The attempt to use and to imagine away religion is as fundamentally mis-conceived as Marxist attempts to imagine it away through false consciousness or through the secular values of the Academy.

I now want to say something about Irish Protestantism, more specifically about Southern Irish Protestantism. Presbyterianism has been the dominant influence on Northern Protestantism, but Anglicanism has largely shaped Southern Protestantism. What I have to say may arise out of the arrogance of ignorance of being a Northern Presbyterian, perhaps out of the antipathy and rivalry between Presbyterian and Anglican which has been an important element in Northern Protestantism, and perhaps out of a spirit of contestation with the ghost of Hubert Butler who has been adopted as Patron Saint of the Conference. Butler, I feel, does not really help in understanding the Southern Protestant tradition, a man who was marginal to that tradition in terms of his rather aristocratic self-conscious Republicanism and whose 'real religion' was a dream of local co-operative community.

The Southern Protestant tradition since the middle of the nineteenth century can, I believe, be understood as one of pain, despair,
disdain, withdrawal, uneasy belonging and, finally, a suppression of
memory. These feelings are part of the explanation for the well-
nigh terminal spinelessness that afflicted the Southern Protestant
community until recently, a spinelessness that did *not* affect Hubert
Butler, I may say, but then he learnt what it cost to step out of line.

I want to begin by quoting from a hymn by Mrs Frances Alexan-
der, the well-known hymn writer who wrote 'All Things Bright and
Beautiful' and was the wife of a Bishop of Derry. It was sung in her
husband's Cathedral the day disestablishment came into force:

> Look down, Lord of heaven on our desolation,
> Fallen, fallen, fallen is now our Country's crown,
> Dimly down the New Year as a Churchless nation,
> Ammon and Amalek tread our borders down.

For those of you who did not go to a Protestant Sunday School, the
Ammonites and the Amalekites were the enemies of Israel, with
whom there were endless battles. Disestablishment marks the start
of Protestant defeat and withdrawal.

A passage from Elizabeth Bowen's book, *Bowen's Court*, illustrates well the ambiguity of the Southern Protestant position of
belonging and not belonging:

> Ireland had worked on them, through their senses, their nerves.
> They had come to share with the people round their senti-
> ments, memories, interests, affinities. The grafting-on had been,
> at least where they were concerned, complete. If Ireland did not
> accept them, they did not know it – and it is in that awareness of
> final rejection [*notice those words*], unawareness of being looked
> at from some secretive, opposed life, that the Anglo-Irish naive
> dignity and, even tragedy seems to me to stem.[2]

There is real pain here – a sense of tradition having ended.
Elizabeth Bowen was writing *Bowen's Court* in the early 1940s. I am
sure that Protestants in the Republic would not say the same today,
but the passage illustrates well the pain that independence and
the British withdrawal brought.

Another illustration of pain is found in Edward Carson's maiden
speech in the House of Lords when he spoke on the Anglo-Irish

Treaty of 1922. It is a bitter threnody, a requiem for an Irish Unionist tradition:

> I speak – I can hardly speak – for all those relying on British honour and British justice, who have in giving their best to the service of the State seen themselves now deserted and cast aside without one single line of recollection or recognition in the whole of what you call peace terms in Ireland.[3]

Carson's tragedy was that he was not an Ulster Unionist but an Irish Unionist; and I think he must have been speaking for many.

And yet much of the memory of this has disappeared. The Anglo-Irish have lost their memory in most part. Whatever memory remains is carried by the Church of Ireland which, to quote Kenneth Milne, a Church historian, 'provided for its members in the difficult and dangerous early days of the Free State a religious and cultural focus, a sort of sheet anchor, a shelter for the Protestant and generally Unionist community'. He goes on to say: 'Somehow in this way, the shift of allegiance was facilitated, though there was much pain, and not a little bloodshed and violence'.[4]

I find a nice symbol for the role of the Church of Ireland in the preservation of the Southern Protestants in the fate of Bowen's Court. Elizabeth Bowen struggled to keep the house going until 1960 when it had to be pulled down. Now only the small Anglican Church in the grounds remains. The big house has gone and only the little Church remains.

Read the novels of Jennifer Johnston. The portrait of the Anglo-Irish is one of lostness; not irredeemable lostness, it is true, but the consequence of communication with the other tradition is often pretty disastrous. Samuel Beckett in his work projects this lostness, this sense of an end of a tradition, out on a cosmic scale.

Has the pain of change led to a suppression of memory or even to an obliteration of memory? Has this in fact been the price of change? Or have the memories gone because they are no longer relevant, because the antagonisms have disappeared, because the ambiguity of the Protestant position in Ireland – at least in the South – has been resolved?

These things should be talked about. Perhaps there is a difficulty for Irish Protestants today to face these things. Perhaps there is a difficulty for the Irish Catholic tradition to face them also. For they challenge a certain repressive tolerance in dealing with other traditions. Rather than take them seriously, let's be nice to them, as long as they fit in.

References:

1. Duncan Morrow, *The Churches and Inter-Community Relationships* (Centre for the Study of Conflict, University of Ulster at Coleraine, 1991).
2. Elizabeth Bowen, *Bowen's Court* (Virago Press Edition, 1984), p 160.
3. Quoted in H. Montgomery Hyde, *Carson: The Life of Sir Edward Carson, Lord Carson of Duncairn* (London: Heinemann, 1953).
4. Kenneth Milne, St Patrick's Day Sermon, Down Cathedral, 1989.

Religious Ireland (III)

SISTER HELENA O'DONOGHUE

Religion as a Cultural Force in a Changing Ireland

In my short contribution this afternoon to this important conference I have chosen to focus on four points, all of which relate to division or diversity and sometimes both! I speak from my own perspective as a woman and as a Catholic, whose experience has been mainly in the South of Ireland. I hope what I share usefully serves the theme of the Conference.

Firstly, I wish to make a distinction between religion and faith. I believe that both of these are commonly fused together in such a way as to be unhelpful in looking at the true role of religion in a society. *Secondly, we are in a time of transition in terms of culture, and of secularisation in terms of religion.* The role of religion in society today is not what it was in the past. *Thirdly, the emergence of a responsible respect for differing viewpoints as a desirable norm in society,* the presence or absence of which contributes very much to division or diversity, is more widely acknowledged among the younger generation. *Finally, the idea of developing a holistic culture* – one which gives freedom and expression to the whole of human aspiration and experience, the deeper metaphysical as well as the more practical/political/economic dimensions of human life and interaction – is critical in the search for peace and harmony among peoples.

Religion and Faith

So, taking the first point of the confusion of religion and faith: To use a common phrase – there is religion and religion in it!. A 'religion' as it is commonly understood, relates very often to a specific church or denomination, a gathering of people with common values and common patterns of worship, common scriptures, and who give expression to these both externally and publicly i.e. the Catholic, the Anglican, the Methodist, the Jewish, the Islamic religions etc. A 'Religion' in this sense is something historical and has a long story with significant events, founders, leaders, and evokes emotion and commitment because of this historical dimension. It is often used as an identity card, as a mode of differentiation from others and even associated with raw nationalism. This form is calculated to create and maintain divisions and we see many instances of that in our own history and in that of other countries both in the past and in the present.

Faith, on the other hand, is something deeper and relates to the individual's personal experience of the phenomenon of God, of the dimension of mystery, of the appropriation of meaning and value in life. It goes beyond the tangible and verifiable and is based on a trust in One greater than the human reality. Faith or spirituality touches the core of one's self-understanding and in the concrete expression of that experience a particular stance emerges which underpins a person's chosen set of values and patterns for life. The individual will then often seek to embody and affirm these values and patterns by connecting with others and it is out of that movement that a specific denomination or 'religion' is formed. The recognition of Jesus of Nazareth as the personification of God in human form has become for many the core meaning of life. The following of this Man resulted in the formation of a group initially known as the Way, later known as Christians and finally as Catholics and Protestants with all their variations, etc. It has had a long two-thousand year history at this point. What I'm saying is that faith ideally precedes religion and that one without the other is incomplete.

However, here in Ireland both North and South, and perhaps elsewhere, 'religion' often comes first and in fact may not be accompanied by any coherent personal faith experience. This is due really to the climate of religious culture we live in, where religion is very often a matter of inheritance, and infant baptism sets so very many of us in a religion before we have reached the point of choosing such as individuals. Religion in this case often does not develop properly through spiritual experience, to ensuing maturity and eventual coherent commitment. Some tenets of a particular religion in this context can become arbitrary absolutes, very much non-negotiable givens, requiring full unquestioning acceptance, while other tenets remain neglected or ignored. I think we can see instances of this in all of the great religions whether it be the question of Rome, or the place of the Bible, or the place of moral patterns such as divorce or whatever. Going to Mass on Sunday faithfully may live alongside indifference to injustice, or even hatred of another denomination.

When we take surveys or polls about religious practice in Ireland the question that comes to me is whether there is any distinction made between these two aspects? Religion may well be something that stays at the surface of one's consciousness whereas faith emerges from a deep and maybe even subconscious experience of the reality of God, and is the motivating power in any consistent practice of religion. If we do not distinguish between these two aspects, do we get a true and reliable picture of the religious dimension of any people's culture? Where religion is being blamed for divisions is it really religion or some shallow look-a-like?

Furthermore I believe that both aspects are on the wane at present. It is an ebb time for religion and faith in Ireland. The flow time will follow as it has in Russia and Eastern Europe. There is danger in the flow – danger of excess and division. There is also danger in the ebb – danger of privatisation and the loss of a sense of concern for social growth and the development of harmony.

Transition
My second point is the fact that we are living through perhaps the greatest time of change in recorded history. So many eras are coming to an end, the industrial age, the mechanistic era, the age of western dominance, of patriarchal patterns and, not least perhaps, as our most recent evidence shows, the end of the socialist era. I think that as a human species in this twentieth century we have moved onto a new level of consciousness in our evolution. This new level has made us more acutely aware than formerly that the state of our world is the result of our own decisions and choices – perhaps the decisions and choices of the few imposed on the many, but nevertheless our own decisions and choices. We are also acutely aware that tomorrow's world will follow from today's decisions as surely as daylight follows darkness, and what people demand now is that they be involved in the decision-making that shapes tomorrow. We are in the age of 'people power' and perhaps media power. In this context all dimensions of life, including religion, are going through a profound metamorphosis. Religions and Churches do not remain static or immune to what is happen-

ing. Both the insider and the outsider need to recognise that the garden of religion is changing fast and we need rigorous honesty and discipline not to be fighting about what is already gone or in the process of going, for that would be terrible waste of human energy. It is a sad fact when traditions and denominations look on each other with anachronistic eyes through timewarp glasses.

One change most notable in the milieu of religion is the disappearance of blind submissive obedience. In a climate which promotes adult responsible participation there is an unwillingness to accept the imposition of regulations or perspectives or theories, or even the withholding of knowledge in religious affairs as much as in any other area. This is borne out in the current debates about moral issues which at present centre around sexuality but which will no doubt involve wider ethical areas of injustice, discrimination and technology-questions in the future. The clarity of church or denominational stances on many issues cannot be presumed to be on tap – it must be sought for through reflection and search.

Another transitional effect is the impact on religion of secularisation in recent decades. This is not necessarily a bad thing as it has modified the division between the sacred and profane. But it does mean that many sacred and long cherished patterns of any particular denomination may not be held on to with the same devotion as members of other traditions might think. The areas of the God-world and non-God-world are not so separate any longer. Where secularism comes to dominate, then the alternatives to religion – consumerism, affluence and individualism – take the foreground and they certainly contribute to many divisions in society.

This transition time also sees the weakening of the role of church structures, especially that of the parish (unless it be at the G.A.A. level) for many Catholics. Greater mobility has contributed to this but also, and perhaps especially for women, the enduring clericalisation of Church structures makes the ideal of parish less and less attractive or relevant. Declericalisation rather than an anti-clericalism is at work in our society. Where no progress is made, an attitude of neutrality and apathy, and even anger, rather than one of commitment and involvement grows. In this context religion could hardly be credited with being strong enough to be very divisive. It lacks the vitality to be so, while a growing diversity, out of personal rather than communal choice, seems to be more evident.

Responsible Respect

My third point relates perhaps to one of the characteristics of maturity which might be described as a 'responsible respect for the viewpoints and values of others' however much they differ from my own. In so far as the churches do not cultivate this responsible respect then the danger of promoting or at least permitting divisions to persist is very real. Culture today is very fluid, is being created all the time, is something organic and living. It is going to be very much affected by the explosion in technology and information, and something like a world culture is very much a reality in contemporary times. There will come a greater realisation that the peoples of the earth are yet only at the brink of understanding the meaning of our planet and our purposes on it. A healthy respect emerges from an awareness that none of us knows it all and that no one denomination or Church has a fullness of understanding. There emerges, too, a recognition of the genuine search that is ongoing and will be ongoing in the human heart and spirit. Churches will be called on to be less paternalist, less dogmatic with the cherished viewpoints and perspectives which they articulate. The right wings and left wings of institutions/religions will be seen either as autocratic or fearful, both approaches at odds with the development of personal responsibility and mutual respect. The zeal of fundamentalists and the fanaticism of right wings are the very elements of religion which will contribute to further divisions in the future and will have nothing to show in terms of the creation of unity that embraces diversity in harmony.

I believe that the quality of responsible respect requires that all denominations analyse their religious language and symbols in order to weed out what is divisive, paternalist, and fundamentalist because all of these aspects create division and retard the co-operative making of God's world. A responsible respect would bring about a new dialogue and a new mutual relationship between denominations in any one country and that could only contribute to peace and to harmony.

Holistic Culture

Finally, culture is not a given, and is not necessarily complete or fully rounded at any one time. Very often we look at our culture and accept willy-nilly its various ingredients, aspects, values, dimensions. But perhaps we also accept it as a rounded reality more than it deserves. We talk about a religious culture or secular culture, but if culture is the milieu of blended values and patterns in which people live and inter-relate, then I believe we need to promote within the notion of culture a holistic approach which would value the spiritual dimension of human reality. The only culture which will contribute to harmony will be one which recognises and promotes the spiritual values of the human species and allows those to be expressed in a variety and a diversity of modes. In Ireland, particularly at this time of transition, many tend to look at what is new and what is evolving as non-religious or as perhaps 'secular'. I believe this is divisive in itself and will contribute to the fragmentation of society and alienation of groups and of individuals from particular religions. A secular culture is not a holistic or humanising one, if it is secular in the sense of wanting to suppress, ignore or neutralise religion, no matter how benevolent that movement is. For to suppress the evolution and expression of the spiritual dimension of peoples, as is now recognised clearly in the changing Soviet society, is to stall and prevent the reach of the human spirit which gropes toward the transcendent. It is to be anti-cultural in the fullest sense.

Conclusion
In any movement seeking to develop co-operation between peoples of different and antagonistic persuasions I think that further exploration of the points I have referred to would yield dividends for greater mutual understanding and the hope of eventual harmony.
Thank you very much.

GENERAL DISCUSSION

Chairman:
I wish to thank the three speakers in this section of the programme, David Stevens, Tom Kilroy and Sister Helena
O'Donoghue. For my part, I was deeply moved by David Stevens'
threnody, his cry of pain in the face of change. The contributions
of Tom Kilroy and Sister Helena demonstrate approaches to the
questions posed by the place of religion in the cultures of this
island, which are very different.

I know that there will be many people present who will wish to
make contributions to this part of the programme, and it is important that we should have a full and open exchange of opinions.
Whilst this subject has been debated many times before, it is
clearly central to our deliberations, and I invite your contributions.

After the debate, I propose with your approval to suggest a
number of ways in which the work we have embarked upon at this
conference might be carried forward into the future. My suggestions will necessarily be tentative and subject to your approval, but
I would like, if possible, to arrive at a consensus about our future
endeavours.

I do not propose attempting to give a summary of the conference. Our work here has really been preliminary and tentative.
What really matters, in my view, is where we go from here, and I
would be most anxious to have your views on that. Accordingly,
after the religious debate I shall attempt to suggest ways forward.

Fergus O'Ferrall:
I think we could start with Tom Kilroy's main theme: fear. Interest-
ingly this has also emerged in Northern Ireland recently in Simon
Lee's paper 'Freedom From Fear' (*see Freedom from Fear: Churches
Together in Northern Ireland* ed. S. Lee, published by Institute for

Irish Studies, QUB, 1990). As Simon Lee suggests, the churches can make a real contribution to reducing 'fear' to which they may well have contributed in the past.

Recollecting Sister Helena's contribution on the theme of faith, it is vital to remember that in the Gospels faith is the opposite of fear. Ultimately faith is the only way to remove fear.

There is an interesting concluding paragraph in a column by Fintan O'Toole in the *Irish Times* analysing liberalism and conservatism in the Catholic Church:

> The most powerful and challenging things that are happening in the Catholic Church are not the attempts of Liberals to alter the message to suit the times, but the determination of those who are confident of the richness of their own tradition to unleash the critical powers of that tradition. There are Catholic priests and nuns and lay people who find in the Gospels, not the confirmation of the way things are now, but a call to arms in the cause of a different sort of society. By ignoring the liberal conservative paradigm, they are also exploding it.

That is my experience also – I work in the National Bible Society of Ireland which serves all churches – and right around the country you find people all the time seeking to go back to the radical message of the Gospel in so many different ways. One way forward for 'Cultures of Ireland' is to seek to build a network with all these people in the different churches with the objective of replacing fear with faith.

Werner Jeanrond (theologian):
I teach theology at Trinity College, Dublin. I am painfully aware that none of us Christians here has resisted enough the exploitation of religion by professional religionists. Tom Kilroy spoke correctly of the widespread fear which is nourished by various kinds of religionists and by their bizarre understanding of both the natural law and the biblical texts. Fear, it seems, is used to maintain a given power-structure in religion. Fear and anxiety, however, are not at the root of the Christian movement. Rather at the very beginning of Christianity stands the 'do not be afraid' of the resurrected crucified Jesus. Yet very sadly, fear still has a hold on many of us. But it is also important to draw attention to the new and constructive initiatives by individual Christians and Christian

groups in Ireland which transcend the boundaries of 'Catholic' and 'Protestant' traditions. Since I came to Ireland ten years ago I have encountered numerous such groups of people who are not motivated by fear of overstepping the marks decreed by their mostly self-appointed leaders, but who are encouraged and brought together by the 'do not be afraid' message of Jesus of Nazareth.

I am very grateful to our three speakers for having slaughtered a number of holy cows which needed to be slaughtered, but I think one has to take the issues further. We need to ask the question whether or not Christianity can still make a constructive contribution to the shaping of the plurality and diversity of this culture. We need to discuss what this critical and self-critical contribution could consist of. I am convinced that Christian faith can make such a contribution, but it must resist all temptations to gain once again an overall political and cultural control over this culture. It seems to me that the best that Christians could do is to enrich the diversity of contemporary Irish culture by presenting without fear their own positive visions of this culture and refrain from any effort to dominate the public conversation on their or any other vision. Either we Christians convince our non- or post-Christian friends and fellow citizens by our willingness to engage critically and self-critically in such a pluralistic and open-ended conversation, or we risk being ignored by them. How can we meaningfully resist any dogmatist trend in our culture if we are not prepared to resist the dogmatists in our own circles and even in ourselves?

Chairman:

Is there any reality in hoping that the church establishments would be able to resist manipulation?

Werner Jeanrond:

My aim was to offer a Christian view which may take us beyond the now given church establishments. The church organisations are good in so far as they lead us to recognise the foundations of Christian faith, to overcome our human fear and to step forward in helping to create a new plurality and diversity in Christianity itself and in this country. If, however, the present church structures are hindering us from making our own constructive Christian contributions to this process of a plural search for truth, then we may have to transform them or even develop new forms of church.

Chairman:
How?

Werner Jeanrond:
First of all by ignoring those church structures which are in our way of responding responsibly to Jesus Christ's creative initiatives, just as Christians do in other countries. As a once foreign observer, who is now increasingly carrying the weight of Irish cultural baggage as well – having spent the last third of my life here – I am still amazed how so many Irish people feel free to exercise great liberty and selectivity in responding to legal arrangements in this country, eg, traffic laws, tax laws, etc, but at the same time cling childishly to the laws of the churches, at least by paying lip service to them, rather than taking a bit of this otherwise anarchic freedom in order to reflect more critically on the church-given laws. The sometimes anarchic nature of Irish society, unfortunately, does not often display its creative impulses in the churches. It may, of course, be that the churches are providing the kind of morality and security network on which we perform our otherwise often anarchic existence. You see, it is not my intention to blame the churches for all the dogmatisms in our own heads. Rather, I would want to encourage everybody to review critically her or his own attitude first. If we do not acquire the God-given freedom to think, to act and to resist, there is no hope.

John Waters (*Irish Times*):
Just one small point on that. There's one particular issue which has brought an awful lot of the different strands in the North and South together recently. I'm not sure of the exact significance of this, but it's the Du Pont incinerator plant in Derry which actually brought people, Protestants, Catholics, Unionists, Nationalists together in opposition. I think it's a very symbolic thing. I think there is a link between that and a subject we have been discussing – the kind of thinking that has gone on in the world has brought us in the opposite direction to that of the natural law. The idea of the environment being despoiled by philosophies which are not being checked by notions of spirituality, solidarity and so on. I think that might be a starting point: that the threat which faces

everybody can in fact be addressed from a common base in the natural law, which is religion and faith.

Edna Longley:
Maybe I'm going to say the same thing as Mary Holland seems about to say – that the other issue which has wonderfully brought the churches together in the North is the Brook Advisory Clinic. So I think that's the other side.

Mary Holland (*Irish Times*):
It's also the natural law, no doubt, that young girls should not be given contraceptive advice. Therefore that unites the churches in not letting them get it, despite the fact that there's an alarming rise in the number of teenage pregnancies. That's why the Brook Advisory Clinic was invited in by the Director of Health in the Eastern Health Board, who is a Catholic.

Brian Walker (Queen's University Belfast):
May I just make a point in response to the criticism that has been made here today against the institution of the church? It's far, far too easy to blame the church authorities. What we also ought to pay attention to are the politicians, and the political ethos which ties together religion and politics. I am often at ecumenical dos, and one finds there clergy together in very good relations, and yet you go outside and there are politicians insisting on certain political lines which tie in very closely with religion. Now we are partly to blame for this, because we allow this culture which ties the two together, and I think part of the value of this conference today is in looking at our culture, seeing the way religion and politics are intertwined, and how they can be torn apart. It doesn't mean, on the other hand, we go for a materialist non-Christian society, because there are other societies in Europe and America which have a strong religious ethos: it just doesn't intrude into politics the way it does here. So I think we shouldn't take the simple line of blaming the church authorities for everything.

Gerald Dawe (poet, Trinity College Dublin):
The thing that has struck me about what Tom Kilroy said, I think actually links together a lot of what we should try to resolve in this afternoon's session. It strikes me that the notion of fear is not monopolised by the Catholic Church. Northern Protestantism has

created that legacy too in the North, needless to say. The problem has always been, I think, the extent to which churches don't want their own members to countenance that which is different, and on the basis of that difference, of refusing to let other people be different, all sorts of political civil rights are denied. In other words, the churches are policed by the politicians who are in turn policed by the church. And maybe one of the things that we ought to clear up, if only in note form by the end of this afternoon's session: is that we can create an agenda today – something along the lines of Charter '88 – whereby we can make a kind of constitutional campaign, one that comes out of the many cultures in Ireland.

Chairman:
Spell that out for us.

Gerard Dawe:
How long have you got? Well, I think Gearóid O'Tuathaigh in his contribution this morning implied a relentless crusade or pursuit whereby we here down in the Republic would rewrite the constitution. I don't see why that should be done with an eye to the North. I think that could be done straight away by those of us who live here, and that would get the ball rolling. There's obviously a very direct moral, spiritual and political connection between people's fear of that which is different and the civic space in which people should be able to move and respect each other. There's a very direct relationship between the two, so unless we can clear one – the fear, the other situation will not be resolved.

James Hawthorne (Chairman, Community Relations Council in Northern Ireland):
I'm one of those tribal Northern Protestants on whom the good seed fell for many years – but on stony ground, increasingly stony ground. And if I may misquote the rest of the verse, the fowls of the air sprang up and choked it. Not a disaster. Religion was choked by many things while my mind was opening to that which years of being 'saved' had failed to reveal. But don't feel sorry for me. I'm extremely happy in my present state and have been for many years. I could go on a bit about how and why I still subscribe to the Church, how I regard it and why I like some elements of it. But there's a point I should like to put to those who defend the Church's position. The standard defence seems to be that it has a core of real truth even though, around that core, is a shell of sham

and imperfection. We are asked not to worry about unexplained mysteries, to ignore the imperfections because there is essential truth that we can believe in. But surely it's a matter of balance. How many imperfections must we put up with before we have doubts that there is perhaps something wrong with the core? Or maybe the core doesn't exist. The case of the Brook Clinic is relevant. I happen to be the Chairman of the Health Promotion Agency of Northern Ireland and, after much research and careful debate, the Agency came to the conclusion that we should back Brook and we did so with conviction in the light of the evidence. You may know perhaps that the clinics have been established in Britain for twenty-seven years. They have, as it were, Royal approval. They have been effective. They are run entirely by doctors and medically trained personnel. Yet two weeks ago, in many churches in Northern Ireland, there was a concerted effort from the pulpit to discredit them. The whole scheme was described as 'murder – murder of children' and churchgoers were asked to take up the leaflets, available at the end of the service. There were instructions how to sign up, write letters and form pressure groups against Brook and the point was made that, if you didn't do what you were being asked, then you were equally guilty of the murder of those children. I think that that is appalling and I really should like to know: is that an example of the shell or the core? I have to say that I don't know what the Fourth Commandment is – I've forgotten – but I rather suspect I've been keeping it for years and, if so, because of a mixture of common sense and human values and so I remain dismayed when, in the name of the Church, there is a concerted attack against a very compassionate and important idea by those who haven't even tried to think it through. And so I repeat my question: are we talking about the core of Church opinion or merely its awesome outward shell?

Chairman:
Now, that's an important question, and it deserves an answer or an attempt at an answer.

Nuala Kernan (architect):
I'll be cheeky enough to answer it. I've been a member of the Laity Commission in the Catholic church for a number of years, and am no longer – my term is up, and I'm kind of relieved because I've been trying to change things at the top and was totally ineffectual.

And now in fact people welcome me back home, and it's much more encouraging. I think it's time that people like us, who want to, take charge of our own lives, because I think it's terribly important for the people who don't have the capacity: either because they don't have enough money, or they don't know how to articulate it, or in some ways aren't empowered. And this has been my experience: I meet a lot of people who don't know how, who one way or another haven't the confidence or whatever it takes, and if someone like me doesn't have the courage to take charge of my own life, how on earth can they be expected to, when they have less abiity to, when they have less power to? I used to say that we lay people in the Catholic church wouldn't even get up to open a window when we went inside that building. Now we have actually improved in twenty years, sometimes I'll open a window or close it. But we literally used to go in and behave as if we were seven year-olds: we could have been managers of industry, or goodness-knows-what, but we behaved like seven year-olds, and to a certain extent we still do.

Or else we behave in a kind of subversive way: where we take charge of our lives, but we don't declare it. Most married people today have taken charge of their own sexuality, but they don't declare it – they just get on with it, and aren't looking for hassle. I'm not to blame them, but at the same time there has to come a point when we talk about it. Womens' groups have been trying to do this, but again women have not been especially powerful, and I think they are trying to articulate what is our actual experience and make it important.

Now to me Christian faith is still important, and I'm damned if I'm going to be pushed out. I'm going to hang in there. I can be a thorn in the side or I can be irrelevant as I've often been, but I'm going to hang in there. And I would like people in Ireland to have the choice. I do realise, with my own children, that it is a choice: I would like them not to feel that, because of the restrictions they are experiencing, they don't have the choice – that if they spoke at all, they would have to get out. I would like that faith – for me that's faith in Jesus Christ, to be presented in such a way that they could choose.

So, I think that the people who are actually experiencing the most fear are the people in authority. I've had a fair bit of dealing with bishops and they absolutely frustrate me, but in a kind of way I can understand. We grew up in a church where we understood that we had a treasure – it was something in a golden box and we mustn't lose it. And they are the men who were brought up this way, and they don't want to be the generation who lost it. And what we have lost is that Gethsemane and death comes before resurrection. We have lost that bit, but we are still holding on to that golden box, and I think if people of faith (not only religious faith) and hope and optimism, however that is expressed in themselves, in their spirits, can only take charge of their own lives, perhaps even the faith of Jesus Christ might live in Ireland.

Sister Helena O'Donoghue:
I would like to comment briefly in response to James Hawthorne's question there, because I brought up the question of core and shell. The example that you gave of what happened in churches, in terms of preaching and some kind of a leaflet, now that to me is an example of a paternalist approach, which could be about any issue. Where you are told what to do and how to do it. Something similar happened to me in Ring: on the fourth commandment, 'Honour thy father and thy mother', the argument was that I wasn't honouring my father and mother if I didn't speak the tongue that my great-great-great-great and all before me may or may not have spoken, because I don't know what my pedigree is, in so very many ways. And I think that it's a church problem, but it's more than a church problem.

To me it's a question of growth of people in responsibility and in action. Now on the particular issue, it's one of the questions that have new implications for us today in a way they didn't have before. And I think it behoves us all, those who think like us, and those who don't like us, to explore the issues with reflection and research, and in the context of a deep understanding of whatever is in the stress, or pain or misery. But the issue of abortion and all of that is bigger than Ireland at the moment, it's one of the world questions for the Church, and it's simplistic to think we have answers about some questions that easily. But I think we need to grow up as people, and it's not just the clergy's fault that we acquiesce in paternalistic attitudes.

But that's a weapon, a fear.

Werner Jeanrond:
Could I just offer one additional comment? Since a number of speakers referred already to the concept of God, I wish to say that the current confusion in religion and any discourse on religion in

Ireland relates to a very monolithic concept of God. The people who presented us with this one-sided concept tried to give the impression that they knew so well what they were talking about. Therefore they were seldom questioned in the past. This is different now. So many people are now searching for a better or more adequate understanding of God, for this 'unknown entity', the 'unknown personality', the 'otherness' of God, or in whatever language the question emerges. In its own theological and literary history (from John Scotus Erigena to Patrick Kavanagh), Ireland shows a remarkable richness and diversity in approaches to God, a diversity which has influenced also Continental European thinking and spirituality. Coming from one of these cultures whose understanding of God has been shaped to a large extent by Irish missionary spirituality, I feel privileged to be able to tell my students about this rich heritage and to remind them, with the best of the Irish tradition of speaking about God, that God is not the puppet to which he has often been reduced by those in religious or political authority, who either did not struggle to find out more about the God of Israel and of Jesus of Nazareth, or who simply may have needed a holy reference for their unholy pursuits.

I do agree with Mary Holland that it is indeed the task of all people involved in education, either at home, in the media, or in schools and universities, to demolish this unchristian image of God, an image used to keep people at bay and to suffocate their creative abilities. We need to bring back to everybody's attention the search for the God of Jesus Christ, who is not a God of terror and retribution, but a God of love and reconciliation whose plan it is to allow us to be fellow creators of his universe and of his reign, the God who supports our search for who we are as persons and as communities. This God of which the Bible speaks wants us to be free, not slaves, and certainly not slaves of any religious system. Our search for the God of Jesus Christ will lead us to re-read the biblical texts and to re-examine the large, but ambiguous Christian tradition of speaking about God.

Joseph Liechty:
I am very sorry Tom Kilroy has gone because I wanted to respond to some things he said. I'll need to make it a point to write to him. On the one hand, in listening to him, I felt at times the most fervent assent: in particular, when he talked about Christianity getting down on its knees before the people of Ireland, to apolo-

gise for what has been done to them in the name of religion. Amen. And I think there is a secularist critique of what Christianity has done that can be very helpful in doing that repenting. Therefore, because I think the secularists have something to offer the Christians, I regretted his ascribing maturity to secularists and childishness to religious people.

First of all, it is tactically a poor way to encourage dialogue. Secondly, I find it unrelated to reality. I don't see this mature, political-only culture anywhere in the world. In fact, the one massive effort to build an exclusively politically based state and culture is collapsing all around us, except in China where it continues its repressive ways. So I can't see that there is a mature/childish distinction that is at all helpful in the discussion between christians and secularists.

What I would say then, recognising the problem of immature religion, that what we should be seeking is not the absolute ascendancy of politics but mature religion. For example, if we can abandon as illusory the idea of simply getting rid of religion as childish, then maybe it's important to redeem some of the religious themes that can be destructive. Tom Kilroy mentioned in particular the idea of the chosen people or elect which can indeed be interpreted most destructively. I have no quarrel with that. However, although I'm no great biblical scholar my understanding is that the notion of election in its deepest and truest biblical sense, has to do not with spiritual privileges to be lorded over others, but with being called to serve God by serving the world.

That's not only a pretty healthy religious vision, but a healthy political vision as well.

James Hawthorne:
Just to clear a point up. I'm not, obviously, against opposition to Brook Clinics. Clearly I would want to respect every view that's held on the contentious area. I think what I was pointing to is the method and the authority of the Church in the guidance of its flock on that issue. I hope that that was clear.

Chairman:
It was clear.

Dermot Lane (Mater Dei Institute of Education):
I was just listening to James there and I'd want to express my unhappiness with the language that we use sometimes when we're

talking about things related to Christianity. Particularly when we say the inner core and the outer shell. Because I think that gives the impression that somebody has access to an inner core and they are in a privileged position to tell us children what to do or not to do. And the only way in which the Christian faith is available to us is in cultural and historical and socially conditioned categories. And I have no doubt, listening to the conversations here today, that there is as much of the inner core of Christianity in this room as there is anywhere else in this island of ours. And what is important is to allow that to come out, in and through dialogue, and in and through an ability to disagree civilly among ourselves, so that we can get at those truths that we cherish, and that we would like to share with each other. So the first point that I would make is that we need to watch our language when we talk about religious categories. And the second one is to make a very strong plea that there would be much more open dialogue under the broad umbrellas, perhaps of faith and culture or religion and culture. And thirdly that it is a great pity that there aren't more representatives from the Churches, so that they could be, not superior participants, but one among many participants in a dialogue of equity amongst us all.

Chairman:
Splendidly put. You are right.

Edna Longley:
I hesitate to say anything as a fairly lay and secular person. But having attended part of the Rerum Novarum conference in Maynooth, I'm very impressed by the groundswell of re-thinking and energy from the grass roots Catholic church, as contrasted with the rigid postures of the Hierarchy.

I thought what David Stevens said about the fears of Northern Protestants was very moving and very accurate, and it chimed with something I heard Brian Lennon say at another conference, explaining that part of Northern Protestant consciousness was this sense of being pushed north-east and over the edge. Brian Lennon also pointed to their hyper-awareness of the condition of the Southern Protestant, and that's particularly in the consciousness of Derry Protestants at the moment, who see themselves as shrinking back to the sea.

But on David's point of differences too. Of course, as regards the different Protestant cultures of North and South, the dominant influence of Presbyterianism in the North was absolutely crucial. I think that Irish Catholics sometimes assume that Protestantism is some kind of monolithic construct because Catholicism is one in theological terms. But there is a cultural distinction at any rate between Northern Catholics and Southern Catholics even though they are one church. I don't know whether Southerners appreciate the extent to which the Catholic church in the North operates, as the Catholic church throughout Ireland did in the nineteenth century, as cultural defence. That is its social and political role and it's very, very difficult to get them to talk about integrated education or even sharing sites for teacher training – the attempt collapsed several years ago. And I just wonder whether within the Catholic church there is any, or should be any, North/South dialogue. Perhaps having a Northern head of the Catholic church in Ireland, having the Primate in Armagh, is rather equivalent to having a Polish Pope.

Terence Brown:
May I ask a question, which comes out of a sense of some personal pain as a Northern Protestant who lives in the Republic, and it is this. I have attended from the late 1970s meetings of this order, at which extraordinarily creative and moving expressions of exploratory Christianity have been put forward. 'Almost thou persuadest me to be a Christian?' But, at key moments when it comes down to my civil liberties, as a citizen of a republic, they are denied me at the behest, it seems to me, of a patriarchal authoritarian church.

Why does that continue? Why is that Protestantism within which I was reared with its Calvinistic, its European intellectual traditions, its sense of rootedness in experience, its response in figures like Bonhoeffer or Barth (in Lutheranism) to Nazism: Why is that, in the broad culture of Ireland and Catholic nationalism, not even known about? Why is it so disrespectfully treated?

Chairman:
And the ancillary question. How can we stop that being so?

Terence:
Rooted equally is my appalled consciousness that the history of Irish Protestantism, whether Anglican or Presbyterian, in relation to Catholicism is abhorrent.

Mari Fitzduff (Community Relations Council, Northern Ireland):
I find myself very moved by what Terence says, and I think it ties up
with something I have been wanting to say. Last night we heard a
conversation between Southerners. I wondered and asked had this
kind of conversation not happened lots of times before? Consistently the answer came back: 'Well, actually no, not really' and it
came to my mind that there was an agenda that Southerners
needed to discuss irrespective of us being here.

I want to say that breaking the silence has been the main task of
groups like ourselves over the last few years. There is a fear of
opening a Pandora's box and of challenging whom you have to
challenge. In our experience in the end the risk has been worth it.
But I wanted to say something else – that I want to go home not
having left people here with the burden of feeling that their
problems need to be addressed in the context of the North. I
think it has been said that there is an agenda here of civil liberties
and of rights that should be addressed irrespective of what happens up North. And don't listen to us when we occasionally say:
'Ah, but the urgency is greater for us, we have death on our
doorstep'. Yes, we do, but the task down here is different at the
moment for you, and in a sense I want to go saying, 'feel free
to discuss that without having always to refer to us'. There is
an enormous task here. I've lived in the South and I've lived in
the North. I'm conscious when I come to the South, that in some
ways I'm strangely more free with more choices when I'm in the
North, despite the chaos and the difficulties that we have up
there.

I have been at conferences where I hear people talk about not
even having choices about schools or ethos or whatever, and I
think that liberty is a fundamental question for Southerners to
address. Yes we have our problems, some we are dealing with and I
hope we will deal more productively with them. But your task and
your energy should be about the need here, and I hope the other
Northerners will join me in agreeing with that.

Dr Mary Henry:

I agree with everything that Mari said. Also, I would like to stress
the loyalty of the Protestant population down here to the State,
and our own desire for involvement in it. In the litany we pray
'God save Mary our President and grant the government wisdom'.
I take great pride in this. Last night I tried to say that it caused me

regret and anger to be excluded due to some supposed lack of Irishness, when I have nothing else.

Andy Pollak (*Irish Times*):
I have been working for the past year as a religious affairs correspondent. I'm not a very religious person myself, but I am very concerned about peace and political reconciliation – all kinds of reconciliation – on this island.

One thing that has struck me about church leaders – and particularly Catholic Church leaders – is their total unwillingness to compromise on any fundamentals in order to help bring about peace and reconciliation in Ireland. I put this to Cahal Daly, whom I greatly admire for his courage and attempts to understand and speak for Northern Protestant fears. His response was that the Church is not in the business of compromise – that is the politicians' business. The Church's business is mediating God's truth. I find that quite appalling: it's in the very areas we are talking about – such as personal morality and education – that change must come about, and these are where the Catholic Church is most resistant to change.

I understand too what Nuala Kernan is saying. The hierarchy is trying to hang on to the locked treasure chest of two hundred years of Irish Catholicism – a period which, as Professor Liam Ryan pointed out, is unique in Catholicism, perhaps in Christianity, as a time when a country was almost 100% faithfully adhering to the Catholic faith. They want to keep that chest locked, they don't want to accept any change. That seems to me to be extremely foolish, and the more intelligent Catholic theologians have also pointed out the foolishness of not coming to terms with the modernising, secularising world, and realising that religion has an essential part to play in that world too.

I'll give one example. I was under the impression, having heard the arguments of Cahal Daly and other people high in the Catholic Church who are against integrated education, that it was against Canon Law. However, the other day a Northern Catholic sent me a list of schools in England which are jointly run by the local Catholic and Church of England dioceses. These are diocesan schools jointly run by the Catholic and Anglican bishops. I am obviously being misled on this, and I wonder in how many other areas Canon Law is being used in this way to resist change, when in fact Canon Law is not the reason for resisting change but something more specific to the leadership of the Irish Catholic Church.

I think this is something Irish Catholics in particular have to address, and it has a lot to do with the problem of fear that Tom Kilroy talks about. I would have liked us to talk a little more about the problem of fear within the Catholic Church, fear within an authoritarian church, a hierarchical church. Perhaps this is something we could come back to at a later conference.

Voice:

There's a term in the Irish language that means 'the beloved priest'. And one such man, who was whitewashing his kitchen ceiling one day in the county from which I come, was interrupted by the Protestant Canon. Sometime later the Curate came in and said: 'Father John you should have finished the kitchen ceiling'. And he said: 'I would have had it finished long ago if it wasn't for the Protestant Canon, but it was the usual old stuff we were talking about'. 'Oh, what were you talking about Father John?' 'We were talking about the apostolic succession, as if it matters a damn'.

I have had a number of experiences like that. The first time at Shannon when I told the Catholic Canon that I was going to ask the Protestant Canon to say Grace, he was really completely taken aback. And without knowing exactly what he was saying to me, he said: 'We're not that long out of the catacombs, we're not that long out of the catacombs' and then he said: 'Oh you're right'. But I would say that that is the historical thought dating back to Penal days. I think we are talking about the past now when we recall those incidents, because the present and future are quite different.

Anthony Clare:

I have been thinking about Terence's question as to why he has been to so many conferences like this and heard such positive expressions about a society in which he could so happily live, and yet when the crunch comes the changes are not there. It does link up with something Tim Pat Coogan said about having the right people at such conferences. You know, if you analyse what people are afraid of, one of the key things, it seems to me, that they are afraid of is change. Interestingly enough, a lot of the people in this room are not afraid of change. And I think about that. The people in this room are not afraid of change because what they conceive of as change seems to them as good as, or better than, what they have now. Other people won't change, who remain fixed. Those, we categorise as foolish or ignorant or clinging on, and some of these applications do apply. But one of the reasons they may not change is they aren't so convinced. Seeing a lot of people apparently excited about the prospect of change but at the moment of change retreating, (as perhaps in recent referenda) is not so paradoxical. As Tom Kilroy said, the sentence that rang for me: at the moment of the greatest opportunity for development, the fear is greatest.

The onus on a conference such as this is to widen the debate so that those people who have most to fear about change have that fear reduced. The clear optimism which most of us have, that whatever happens to Ireland is in the end of the day going to be for its better, has to be transmitted. It is not an obvious fact. The interesting thing about the Hierarchy is they have a vision that change is not a good thing. They have a proud vision already of Ireland as Catholic and committed and passionate and good – hence the references to the G.A.A. Final and the singing and so on. They are far from convinced that the changes that are articulated around this room are for the better. I don't have any difficulty understanding why the Hierarchy holds the position it does. People in the churches or people outside the Brook clinic will act the way people here clearly would wish them to act. They are convinced that what they do will eventually be for their betterment and what helps them do that is several things. One is the realisation that what they believe is believed more widely – that they are not isolated or ignorant and that they are not risking this treasure that is referred to, which is a profound belief. It is not just the Hierarchy that is terrified, that what could happen might not be a golden era, but might indeed be a dark age. It lurks in the hearts and minds of many people in this country. They are far from convinced. They are fearful about the future. And the very fact that occasionally we have to be euphoric about the future and convince ourselves about the future suggests that we too cannot be certain – we cannot be sure. We do not know what it will be, and that in itself is an act of faith. I would say to Terence that the reason is: confidence about change has not yet circulated widely enough for it to be transmitted into behaviour and then into change.

Voice:
Just to follow up on what Dr Clare has said . I think we did have a moment of hope in the election of Mary Robinson, which went

against the expected notions of all the various establishments in society. So I believe that the people, and I'm talking about the people as a nation or society, can actually enshrine in their own laws, and their own institutions, what they want. Even against the tides, or even in the presence of various fears.

And I think that the fears in those cases came from very different places than religious places .

So I would just like to say in the context of the conference, that we may be working towards some kind of unity and diversity out of that. I think it would be possible to place in legislation a theme that meets different people's convictions but that people can live happily with. But it's not just the churches. It's a national social problem that we haven't arrived at accepting that kind of diversity so that it could be expressed in our laws. I totally agree with Andy Pollak. So many things that are taken to be dogmatic aren't so. And also very many things that we cherish, views of any one persuasion, do not necessarily have to be enshrined in political legislation. That's what we have to move towards and to have more people at these kinds of gatherings.

David Stevens:

I suppose what I would want to say is that the South is a very rapidly changing society and Irish Catholicism, which is a largely historical construct of the nineteenth century and existed from about the 1870s to the 1960s, is breaking up. Protestantism is also largely a Victorian construct as well and it too is breaking up. And it is clear that we are moving into very different worlds. I think that that is a challenge for Christians. Maybe an appropriate response is to quote Herbert Butterfield: 'Hold fast to Christ and for the rest remain unattached'.

The other thing that I would want to say is I think it is characteristically Irish to endlessly blame Hierarchies. My experience of bishops is that they are people who are trapped. They are trapped by change, they are trapped by the community, the faith communities that they are part of. And the conclusion that I have come to, from a long involvement of working for the institutional church, is that it is only when Christian communities change that leaders will change. It will be by people changing at the grass roots that leadership will be unfrozen. So I think there is a characteristic Southern disaffected Catholic blaming of the bishops which I find profoundly unproductive. I come from a tradition in which congregations very often drove out ministers, the so- called people in authority. I am profoundly sceptical of groups of people who because they have one perception of truth can drive out people who have different perceptions of truth – that's my Protestant Presbyterian background. I feel that a lot of the blaming bishops is actually scapegoating. I think that people should take responsibility for their own faith in many ways and not blame bishops. As we change, others will change.

Voice:

I feel that some of these groups, Family Solidarity and others, will ultimately be a disaster for Christian faith in this country . It will lead to a greater and even more catastrophic polarisation of the community, because power breeds counter-power, and when people see the use of political power by churches ultimately they will be sickened. The lesson for Christian faith is that we follow a person who was abandoned at the Cross – there was no-one except a few women around – and if we follow the way of power as Christian churches, we will destroy ourselves. There are already so many people in this room disaffected by what they see as power and what Christ, I think, wants, is followers not defenders.

We do not need the Family Solidarity people, we need Jesus Christ, which may mean saying no to abortion, but which does not mean trying to coerce people. If we follow the way of coercion, then we are going to profoundly lose, because there is a secularisation of this society going on apace and it will grow if will follow that way of trying to defend religion.

John Wilson Foster (University of British Columbia):

I have come 6000 miles for the conference. I am a Canadian Unionist. And I think it has been worth it. I just want to say this. I think that David Stevens is right – the Republic of Ireland is changing in a number of ways. But the Unionist over the border, who is claimed as a citizen against his will by the Government of Ireland, looks across the border and wants to see these changes translated into hard currency. He doesn't see that at the moment, so I think this conference, the message of this conference is an urgent one. I think yes, cultural diversity, but not cultural diversity in the sense that it is legitimately and rightly interpreted in Northern Ireland – education for mutual understanding and cultural heritage. I think diversity should go forward as a message urgently if it means the diversification of the culture already here in the South. And I think there is an obligation on the part of people who care about Ireland to make of the South of Ireland, other things being equal, a society that can make Terence Brown a happy man.

CONCLUSIONS AND SUGGESTIONS

CHAIRMAN

Our conference is drawing to a close, and I suggest that the time has come to look at the way forward and to try to agree upon some concrete steps which we might take in the light of our discussions to further our aims.

My suggestions are not comprehensive and there will be an opportunity to discuss them and enlarge upon them, if you so desire. My aim is to see if we can arrive at a number of conclusions and suggestions that might go forward as the consensus of the conference.

Firstly, I believe that it is agreed that we should urge the British government, the Department of Education, the universities and other bodies in the country – particularly those concerned with education – that there is a need in this state for an element in school and university syllabuses similar to the 'Education for Mutual Understanding' programme in Northern Ireland. This programme would be aimed at improving the understanding and the relationship between people of different cultural traditions in these islands, including understanding of the nature of the conflicts and tensions between them. It is contemplated that the programme would be inserted into subjects such as history, religious education, civics, literature and languages, and would be preceded by an adequate training programme for teachers to equip them to teach the new material.

Secondly, we appear to agree unanimously that we should urge the same authorities to encourage educational and other bodies to recognise the need for education in cultural heritage, so that those elements of our cultures which are inherited are as widely understood as possible in all their plurality and complexity. Cultural heritage courses are becoming common in the universities and adult-education institutions and training-bodies in many European countries. There is a deep need for them here, and now.

The establishment of such courses would be a progressive step, and a step particularly relevant to our situation.

Thirdly, I think we agree that we should ourselves be considering ways in which the cultures of Ireland could be sustained and further investigated after our conference has ended. One concrete proposal, which I believe has met with your approval, is the suggestion that our purposes could be served by the publication of a periodic journal devoted to Irish culture in all its complexities and diversities.

Hubert Butler proposed such a magazine after the demise of the *Bell* in 1954. He thought it might be called *The Bridge*. In a draft editorial he wrote: 'The Bridge is thrown across the border because something of the kind is needed. It is manufactured in Southern Ireland, assembled for publisher's reasons in the North, it is quite small, it cannot take much traffic, but all who sincerely want to see the other side are invited to use it. It is a movable bridge, and when we have had some experience with the border, we'll try it across some other chasms and obstacles as well.

I am suggesting that we try to follow up this suggestion and supply the very serious lacuna which Hubert Butler identified. What I have in mind is the publication of a monthly or perhaps a quarterly magazine which would, at a high level of intelligence, discuss the problems with which we are concerned and allow them to be discussed by others, so that we can reach out to an ever widening audience.

The next need which I believe we have identified is the need to extend the conversation which we have been having at our conference to young people. We also need to include in our discussions people from other classes and educational attainments, and indeed people of no formal educational attainment. How we reach out to workers and the unemployed requires thought, but urgent thought. We must reach out with thought, sensitivity, intelligence, commitment and respect. I believe that we should plan, or ask our sponsors to plan, a conference at which the young would be encouraged to interrogate those in power, those who hold themselves out as being entitled to make decisions. Such a conference could be put in hand as a matter of urgency.

You appear to me to be of a mind that we should press the Irish government to open up the whole subject of votes for Irish people in Britain. One of the things that we have clearly identified here is the belief that emigrants are an integral part of the complex which is Irish society.

I believe that you would also wish to press the Irish government and the British government for financial support, and generous financial support at that, for the British Association for Irish Studies and for the School of Irish Studies at Liverpool University. Both of these valuable institutions are under-funded to the point where their very existence is at risk. I believe that these institutions are unique conduits for our understanding of the interconnection between Irish and British experience, and I believe that all of us in Ireland need to know and understand this interconnection and its complexities.

It is clear from the debate on religion which we have had that perhaps the most pressing need is to stimulate openness and dialogue with theologians and those in power in the churches. It seems to me to be clear that many of the problems which have been identified at this conference are fundamental theological questions which have never been adequately addressed in the specifically Irish context or in the context of Ireland as it now is. Problems of human liberty, problems of respect for other religions, problems about the Christian faith itself, and about power and inequality, have all emerged. One of the problems that emerged most clearly from the conference is the problem presented by the part that fear plays in the lives of all of us.

These matters could appropriately be the subject of a conference in the form of a major seminar of theologians from all traditions and leaders of all churches of all traditions. Such a conference might consider the initiation of a theological dialogue on these and related questions.

There are, of course, many other things that we could do. The suggestion which appeared to me to commend itself to you is the possibility that we could establish committees from the participants in this conference and other like-minded people who could deal with various specialised subjects and report back to a future conference or to the organisation. These committees might concern themselves with specific subjects such as education, local history, constitutional changes, the further development in twinning towns in the Republic with towns in Northern Ireland. But these are only a few of the many possibilities which I now mention because they were specifically identified.

I would suggest that anyone who is interested in establishing such committees might contact Constance Short, and I am sure a start can be made immediately.

These are some thoughts on a possible way forward. They are my thoughts and mine alone, but derived from what I have been hearing from you at this conference. You will have an opportunity to discuss them.

I wish to thank our sponsors, who made this conference possible. [See following page]

In conclusion, I would say this. Yesterday evening I was in despair about the course the conference was taking. I thought the conference had got off the ground on the wrong foot. It wasn't going to be able to grapple with the essential questions in a sufficiently serious way. I blamed myself for being an overly indulgent chairman. Now, I am not sure that my fears were well-grounded. I think it may be that yesterday we did succeed in breaking the ice. If we broke the ice yesterday, perhaps we succeeded in breaking the silence today. If we have broken the silence, our work has been worth while.

Thank you. I am honoured to have been your chairman.

BIOGRAPHIES

SPEAKERS

Terence Brown
Associate Professor of English at Trinity College Dublin, author (most recently) of *Ireland's Literature.*

Jennifer Johnston
Novelist, author (most recently) of *The Invisible Worm.*

Brendan Kennelly
Poet, Professor of English at Trinity College Dublin, author (most recently) of *The Book of Judas.*

Thomas Kilroy
Formerly Professor of English at University College Galway, dramatist and novelist, a director of the Field Day Theatre Company.

Helena O'Donoghue
President of the Major Conference of Religious Superiors.

Gearóid O'Tuathaigh
Professor of History at University College Galway, co-author of *The Age of De Valera.*

Mary Robinson
President of Ireland.

David Stevens
Assistant Secretary to the Irish Council of Churches.

CHAIRPERSONS

Anthony Clare
Director of St Patrick's Hospital, Dublin, and Clinical Professor of Psychiatry at Trinity College Dublin, formerly head of Department of Psychological Medicine at St Bartholomew's Hospital, London, writer and broadcaster.

Edna Longley
Professor of English at Queen's University Belfast, author of *Poetry in the Wars* and an editor of the *Irish Review.*

Patrick MacEntee (Conference Chairman)
Senior Counsel and Queens Counsel, an internationally-known defence lawyer.

Mr Justice Niall McCarthy
Judge of the Supreme Court and a senior figure in the judiciary of the Irish Republic.

Margaret MacCurtain
Lecturer in Modern History at University College Dublin, author of *Tudor and Stuart Ireland*, Dominican sister and former prioress of Sion Hill Convent.

ACKNOWLEDGEMENTS

For their encouragement and assistance, whether financial or in kind and in some cases both, in the putting together of this conference and this book, Constance Short and Edna Longley wish to thank most sincerely:

Mary Robinson, *President of the Republic of Ireland, our patron*
Charles Haughey TD An Taoiseach, *for endorsing our conference by sending Mr Chris Flood TD, Minister of State to the Department of Health, to represent the Irish Government*
The International Fund for Ireland
The Ireland Funds
Co-Operation North
The Irish Association
The Calouste Gulbenkian Foundation (*Lisbon*)
The Department of Foreign Affairs (*Republic of Ireland*)
The Foreign Office (*United Kingdom*)
The British Council (*Dublin Office*)
The Central Community Relations Unit (*Stormont, Northern Ireland*)
The Community Relations Council (*Northern Ireland*)
The Conference Speakers, Chairpersons and Reporters
The Cultures of Ireland Group *who planned and decided on the content of the conference programme, and conference organisers* **Project Planning** *who pulled it all into shape*
All participants *in the conference*
Deborah Orme, *audio-typist*

Thanks are due to Faber and Faber and to the estate of Louis MacNeice for permission to quote from his poem 'Dublin'.